Teaching for Experiential Learning

Five Approaches that Work

Scott D. Wurdinger
and Julie A. Carlson

ROWMAN & LITTLEFIELD EDUCATION
A division of
ROWMAN & LITTLEFIELD PUBLISHERS, INC.
Lanham • New York • Toronto • Plymouth, UK

KH

Published by Rowman & Littlefield Education
A division of Rowman & Littlefield Publishers, Inc.
A wholly owned subsidiary of The Rowman & Littlefield Publishing Group, Inc.
4501 Forbes Boulevard, Suite 200, Lanham, Maryland 20706
http://www.rowmaneducation.com

Estover Road, Plymouth PL6 7PY, United Kingdom

British Library Cataloguing in Publication Information Available

Library of Congress Cataloging-in-Publication Data
Wurdinger, Scott D.
 Teaching for experiential learning : five approaches that work / Scott D. Wurdinger and Julie A. Carlson.
    p. cm.
 Includes bibliographical references.
 ISBN 978-1-60709-367-1 (cloth : alk. paper)— ISBN 978-1-60709-368-8 (pbk. : alk. paper)—
ISBN 978-1-60709-369-5 (electronic)
 1. Active learning. 2. Experiential learning. 3. Motivation in education. I. Carlson, Julie. II. Title.
 LB1027.23.W86 2010
 371.39—dc22   2009041567

Printed in the United States of America

10/07/10

Contents

Preface

The idea for this book originated years ago, emerging from our work as faculty members in the Experiential Education Master's of Science program at Minnesota State University, Mankato. Scott was the instructor for courses such as "Philosophy of Experiential Education" and "Experiential Learning and Educational Reform." Julie was beginning to regularly offer a course titled "Trends and Issues in Experiential Education." We discovered that we both desired and had been searching for texts that were appropriate for the courses we were teaching, but weren't satisfied with what we had to choose from.

Since undergraduate degrees specific to experiential education are rare, the people who enter our Master's program come from a variety of academic backgrounds. Although many of them are experience-rich in one or two areas of experiential education, they are often lacking in understanding of the field's theory and the full scope of its many approaches. Therefore, it was not unusual, we discovered, for us to spend the first few weeks of our classes getting everyone up to speed, so to speak, with an overview of the field. As we shared some of our challenges and common experiences in our courses, we found ourselves sometimes surmising that we should just write the book we needed ourselves, since it didn't seem to exist.

Eventually, our surmising turned into an actual acknowledgment that the book was needed and we made the decision to begin the project. After several months of Scott's continual encouragement, the book finally came to fruition, with our renewed excitement increasing with every completed chapter. The final product is quite in line with what we had originally envisioned years earlier—a book that is equally user-friendly for new educators, seasoned educators, and educators-in-training.

WHO THE BOOK IS FOR

Although this book was written with our own graduate students in mind, the actual audience for this book is quite broad. It was written by educators for educators from all perspectives—traditional, progressive, and alternative. It is for use with learners of all ages—elementary, secondary, higher education and other adult learners. It is for education in many settings—public, private, judicial, at-risk, therapeutic, community, formal, or informal. Although it is for both inexperienced and experienced educators, it will be most useful for those who are fairly new to using experiential learning strategies, or who are familiar with only a few of the approaches offered herein.

This text was intended to be a book with enough information for conceptual understanding but not so much as to be theoretically overwhelming; a book with enough guidance for getting started but not so much as to be precisely prescriptive; and a book with just enough ideas to generate more ideas without stifling creativity.

HOW THE BOOK IS ORGANIZED

Although we work with an experiential education Master's program, discussions abound among our students, colleagues, and faculty in other disciplines as to what is meant by *experiential education*—what it is and what it is not. Therefore, the need for an introductory chapter with our explanation of how we view experiential education and learning was requisite. This introductory chapter, written by Scott, also identifies the great needs that exist in our current educational systems to reach learners of today in relevant ways, and explains how he came to be passionate about making a difference through experiential learning.

Chapters 2 through 6 provide in-depth probes into five overlapping teaching approaches for experiential learning: active learning, problem-based learning, project-based learning, service-learning, and place-based learning. We chose these five as approaches that are the most appropriate and useful for educators who are fairly new to using experience-based strategies. Each chapter is presented in a consistent, easy-to-read format, first providing various descriptions and definitions of each approach. Each chapter then provides the history of the approach, describes the research base, suggests ways for using and maximizing the approach, and finishes with a list of resources for educators that will lead them to more information and provide them with helpful teaching tools.

These five chapters are intentionally sequenced to gradually build upon each other, each providing another layer of the information previously given. This is important to us because these five approaches are often not used in isolation. For example, a service-learning experience at a local Native American commemorative park repairing vandalized sculptures may embrace active-learning, problem-based, project-based, and place-based approaches all together. At the same time, we wanted to provide chapters that could stand on their own if needed so that educators can easily turn (or return) to the approach in which they are most interested.

Chapter 2 presents active learning (engaging learners in nonpassive ways), which is present throughout all of the other approaches offered in the book. Chapter 3 is focused on problem-based learning, followed by chapter 4 on project-based learning. These two approaches are very closely related because the idea for a project is often born out of a perceived problem or need. Similarly, chapter 5 on service learning and chapter 6 on place-based learning logically follow because both use active learning, and may entail problem-solving or project-based learning. Chapter 7, the final chapter, provides ideas and suggestions for ways to assess the various approaches of experiential learning.

ACKNOWLEDGMENTS

There are some specific individuals who helped in this endeavor whom we need to thank profusely. Jennifer Rudolph and Monica Lunt conducted some of the early research of the literature. Parts of their research also played out in other publications that were pieces of the larger book project. At the time, they were both graduate assistants in our department working on their Master's in Experiential Education. We are hopeful that they learned much in the process, but fully acknowledge the drudgery of research overload that was probably prevalent for them at times. We are indebted to them for all they contributed.

This book would not have been—could not have been—what it is without the continual feedback we receive and the learning we gain from the graduate students we work with. As it should be with experiential learning situations, we are often unsure of who is learning more from whom. Their need for this book *(the learning we hope they will gain from it)* has always been the motivation for this project, and they fueled that motivation unknowingly.

We would also like to thank our colleagues and dean for the freedom and support they provide to pursue these types of applicable and worthwhile projects. The encouragement from our families is omnipresent and confirming. Lastly but substantially, we thank the people at Rowman and Littlefield Education for their help and support in seeing the book through to completion. Specifically, gratitude goes to Thomas Koerner, Vice President and Editorial Director, and Maera Stratton, Editorial Acquisitions, for believing in and fully approving the project.

Chapter One

The Need for Experiential Learning

There are numerous educators both in K–12 and higher education settings doing outstanding jobs motivating and inspiring students to learn. These individuals are hard working, stay abreast of tools and techniques to improve their practice, take risks by testing out new ideas in the classroom, and are extremely dedicated to promoting student learning. The education system however, makes it challenging for these educators to pursue and implement teaching strategies that increase motivation and inspire students to learn.

Research articles and books about exemplary schools and educators who are raising test scores that meet or exceed the No Child left Behind (NCLB) benchmarks are plentiful, but should raising test scores be the primary goal for all schools in the United States? What about helping students become effective problem solvers? What about helping them become team players? What about helping them become self-directed learners? What about inspiring students to become lifelong learners?

Hundreds of books discuss teaching strategies, this one included, that provide specific instruction on how to be an effective educator. Unfortunately, many of these focus on a teacher directed approach where teachers are in front of the class telling students what they need to remember for their quizzes and tests. Direct instruction is necessary at times; however, students become quickly disengaged when teachers do all the talking and do not allow any active participation in classrooms.

We have been teaching in higher education for several years and are discouraged when we listen to students tell their stories of *how* they were taught, mostly through passive methods of learning. The same theme surfaces: they listen most of the time, and when they are allowed to talk it is to answer a question. When asked how they feel about such experiences they use terms such as bored, oppressed, devalued, and ripped off.

On the other hand, we are inspired when we listen to them tell stories about their experiences of when they were most engaged with learning. Examples include fieldwork outside the classroom, discussion and interaction with teachers and students, challenging each other's ideas and practices, and doing meaningful work that can be implemented in real world settings. These stories provide anecdotal evidence, which emphatically supports the notion that students are most excited about learning when they are actively involved in the learning process through discussion, group work, hands-on participation, and applying information outside the classroom. There appears to be a huge chasm between how students like to learn and how teachers teach.

As we routinely walk through the halls of our campus buildings, we often observe professors lecturing in front of their classrooms to groups of disengaged students. Blackburn, Pellino, Boberg, and O'Connell (1980) discovered that 73–83 percent of the 1,800 faculty surveyed chose lecture as their primary method of instruction. In a more recent publication, Huba and Freed (2000) state that most college faculty teach using the lecture method, but their research indicates that other methods are more effective in motivating students to learn. We suspect that the percentage of faculty using lecture as their primary format is still in the majority.

The average attention span of college students is 15 to 20 minutes (Hoover, 2006; Middendorf and Kalish, 1996) so it is no wonder the students we observe in these classrooms are text messaging, working on their laptops, and in some cases sleeping in the back rows. Astin (1993); Levine and Cureton (1998); Sax, Keup, Gilmartin, Stolzenberg and Harper (2002); and Schroeder (1993) all mention in their research on higher education that educators rely heavily on lecture and passive methods of learning, whereas students prefer active methods. Doctoral programs typically do not require students to take any pedagogy courses so it is no wonder that professors continue to teach the way in which they were taught and students continue to be disengaged from what the professors are saying.

We are not entirely against lecturing. We like to attend a good lecture and it should be one of the tools in the educator's toolbox. However, we are against it when it is the only tool, and against it if the only purpose it serves is to dole out information for the next exam. Lectures should be used to help students understand theories, which they can then go out and test against reality during the course, or immediately after the course, to discover whether these theories and ideas have any validity. Otherwise, they may forget the information if they are not allowed to apply it until a distant date in the future.

According to Astin and Oseguera (2002) the national five-year rate of college baccalaureate completion is less than 50 percent, which may be partly due to the use of passive methods of learning. Levitz, Noel, and Richter

(1999) identify multiple reasons why students drop out including academic, social, economical, and personal; however, one reason is that students "experience poor or indifferent teaching" (p. 40). They suggest that a cultural change needs to occur in colleges, which includes faculty becoming more student-centered, thus allowing the students more opportunity to actively participate in the classroom.

College students go through a phase called "focused exploration" (Shaller, 2005, p. 21) which is when they attempt to determine what they want to do with their lives, and opportunities such as "studying abroad, service learning, cooperative learning, internships, and conducting observations outside of school" should be provided Unfortunately, Shaller says many students instead find themselves sitting in large lecture halls disengaged from learning during this crucial phase in their lives.

High school education is also in need of change. Legislators in the United States continue to try and fix a faltering education system without much success, and continue to offer ideas on how to improve the NCLB legislation. Unfortunately, the underlying principles behind NCLB promote a teacher directed approach to learning where teachers dole out information and are held accountable by how well their students perform on high stakes tests.

We live in a democratic society, yet NCLB is not democratic, it's authoritarian. Neither teachers nor students participate in any type of democratic process to determine whether this approach is meaningful and useful. NCLB, which forces teachers to rely heavily on *teaching to the test*, does not provide students with opportunities to discover or explore ideas. The facts to be learned have been identified and the way to assess student achievement is through how many correct answers they can remember for the test.

High school seems to be a significant transition point when students receive more passive methods of learning in the classroom. Discussions with elementary and middle school teachers have led us to believe that these teachers use active methods of learning because their students are in developmental stages where they need to be active participants in the learning process; whereas high school teachers rely on the lecture format because it is more efficient in helping students do well on tests.

However, according to some researchers, even middle school teachers place too much emphasize on lower level cognitive skills at a time when students are in a stage of naturally developing higher-order thinking skills (Cauley and Jovanovich, 2006; Eccles and Wigfield, 1997). Martin (2005) conducted a study on cognitive strategies used by high school social studies students and discovered that lower level strategies, such as repeating information over and over in one's head, are used frequently by students in classes with teachers that lecture. Unfortunately, the lecture format results in the use of lower level thinking strategies, which do not motivate or inspire students to learn.

Some legislators support the development of new schools with different curriculums and approaches to education that do inspire students to learn. Many of these schools are charter schools that have an entrepreneurial flare. Some are theme based and focus on a specific subject area such as science, technology, engineering, or performing arts. Other charter schools utilize innovative approaches to learning such as project based learning and internships. Currently, in the state of Minnesota there are 69 charter schools using experiential approaches to learning that are serving approximately 9,500 students so change appears to be occurring at least in this state (Minnesota Department of Education, 2008).

However as a whole, high school education in the United States is facing a dire situation. According to Greene and Winters (2006), approximately 30 percent of school students who start high school today do not finish. Not only are the lower performing students leaving school; high performing students are disinterested with their education as well.

In *The Silent Epidemic: Perspectives of High School Dropouts*, Bridgeland, DiIulio and Morison (2006) declare that 88 percent of dropout students surveyed had passing grades (p. 3), and about 50 percent left school because they were bored (p. iii). Wolk (2001) cites similar findings in which students chose *boring* as the number one word that best described their school experience and *nothing* as the word that described what they liked best about school. Students' attitudes seem to have changed little over the past decade; however, today they are acting on their dissatisfaction by actually dropping out of school. Could the high dropout rate in college and high school be in part due to an ineffective teaching methodology and an overemphasis on test taking?

One of the authors of this book once attended a high school curriculum advisory committee meeting and was handed a report containing information about various standardized tests students were required to take in the local school district. The number was overwhelming. The chair of the curriculum committee mentioned that the upper class students figured out which tests count for college entrance and which don't, resulting in a situation where they do poorly on state mandated tests, and much better on college entrance tests. Gardener (1991) is correct in stating that, "In the course of their careers in the American schools of today, most students take hundreds, if not thousands, of tests. They develop skill to a highly calibrated degree in an exercise that will essentially become useless immediately after their last day in school" (p. 216).

It is not just students taking tests; teacher candidates and teachers take them as well. Passing one or more pre-professional skills tests (PPST) is required of teacher candidates, as well as veteran teachers from other states wishing to obtain licensure in the state of Minnesota. Education is one of the few fields where tests inundate the system from top to bottom. Educators have been inculcated with testing throughout their entire lives, which may be one reason why this pattern continues.

Educators may find it difficult to move beyond this confine, failing to realize there are other ways to measure student achievement and future potential besides testing. In the past testing was used primarily to measure student achievement; today, however, it is used not only for that purpose, but also as a performance criteria to hold teachers and schools accountable.

The NCLB legislation and the reauthorization of the Elementary and Secondary Education Act forces high schools to perform well on state mandated tests or run the risk of losing their funding (Heinecke, Curry-Corcoran, and Moon, 2003). Teachers are caught in the middle, and even though they may prefer using active methods they fall back to lecturing when state mandated tests are looming in the future. Teachers have shared with us that they use active methods during the semester but switch to lecturing two or three weeks prior to testing time. Many educators know from experience that lecturing is less effective, but their backs are against the wall.

Bill Gates states that if one wants to observe innovation in education one must look at the charter high schools. Both the Bill and Melinda Gates Foundation and the George Lucas Foundation are funding charter schools across the country that use a variety of innovative approaches to teaching and learning. Lucas (2007) states "school life should become more like real life, with school work organized around projects rather than text books, and students working in teams rather than alone" (p. 25). A computer giant and a movie director, neither of whom have a background in education, are spearheading real change in education.

Interestingly, in a lengthy research report titled *Influence: A Study of the Factors Shaping Education Policy* (National Commission on Teaching and America's Future [NCTAF], 2006) eleven of the twelve most influential people who have the greatest impact on educational policy in the United States are outside the field of education. The lone current academician, Linda Darling-Hammond from Stanford University's School of Education "has built a reputation as a leading scholar and expert in educational policy and practice" (p. iv) and was the executive director of the NCTAF from 1994 to 2001. The other eleven are politicians and entrepreneurs.

The field of education might be wise to take some pointers on innovation and creativity from these entrepreneurs. Current policies and practices do not promote innovation and creativity, they promote the status quo and are so tightly woven into the fabric that educators may have a difficult time moving beyond the confines created by this system. Here are a few examples.

- A colleague is a principal at an elementary school in Wisconsin, and received a significant grant to develop a project-based online charter school. School administrators were in support of the project, and my colleague agreed to oversee the new school without any extra compensation. Shortly after a board meeting the superintendent told him to end the project because the board would not support it. Our colleague is innovative, creative, and identified a real need for a specific population of students in his community. He was motivated to carry out the project without pay because he saw a need to help students succeed academically in his community. Unfortunately, what is in the best interest of the child is not always in the best interest of the school system. In this situation the system did not support creativity and innovation. It promoted apathy and it is no wonder that my colleague has decided to do only what is expected of him and work less rather than more.

- A local high school teacher explained that he knows active methods are more effective than lecture in getting students motivated about learning, but he will not use active methods because they are impractical and require more time to facilitate. The amount of curriculum he needs to cover in a semester does not allow him any time to do activities. He said he will continue to use lecture because it is the most effective way to help students do well on the NCLB tests. Unfortunately, it does not matter to this teacher if students are bored and are not enjoying their schooling, as long as they do well on the tests. Furthermore, he realizes that active methods are more effective but fails to recognize that involving students in the learning process allows them to become emotionally invested and motivated to continue learning. He is doing just enough so that students pass their tests and that is it—nothing more. The system once again is promoting an environment where learning is the equivalent of remembering information.

- Tenured full professors sometimes lose motivation and do the minimum amount that is required of them. We have observed professors who live strictly by the union contract covering their courses and office hours and that is it. The system is designed in such a way that by the time professors become tenured and at the top of their pay scale, they are tired of doing research, writing, teaching, and university service. Once tenured, they throttle back on their workload. In addition, there is no pay incentive to work harder. The system does not reward individuals for publishing more articles, increasing enrollments in classes, or serving on more committees. Why work harder when the pay is the same? Like K–12 education, the higher education system has a strong tendency to promote apathy and the status quo.

Systems that do not encourage innovation and creativity have a tendency to stagnate and wear individuals down to the point where they lose desire to do anything new or different. Rigid systems stymie creativity and innovation because individuals are busy concentrating their efforts on following the policies and procedures, which in turn minimizes the amount of time they have for creative thought and action. The inordinate amount of educational policies created by legislators and administrators implies that teachers and students are not capable of being self-directed innovative teachers and learners.

Over time a rigid education system may create rigid employees who become more concerned with following rules than with what the students are actually learning. In some cases this may lead to a negative view of students who are unmotivated and trying to *cheat the system*. For instance, at a college curriculum meeting one of the authors of this book proposed a doctoral level course where the emphasis would be on student publishing and presenting. One member on the curriculum committee raised a question about whether these students would be capable of publishing articles and presenting workshops at conferences. She was assuming these activities would be too challenging for doctoral students. The following response was stated to her, "we have master degree students publishing articles and presenting workshops so I think doctoral students can handle this as well." If they can't do it at the doctoral level, when can they?

Over our careers, we have listened to educators, many unintentionally, undermine student potential. Some educators appear to view students as incapable of being self-directed learners and are in need of external motivators. At what point do educators allow students freedom to become innovative learners? Why aren't educators challenging students more often? What are educators afraid of? What we need are more schools and educators that promote creativity and self-directed learning. Educators need to break the mold and think differently about how they teach.

Five teaching approaches that intentionally promote experiential learning where students are actively engaged in the learning process are *project based learning, problem based learning, service learning, place based education, and active learning*. These approaches have stepped outside the confines of traditional education and are creating new learning environments that are changing the way students, educators, and individuals outside the field of education view learning. They all incorporate student-centered learning, which encourage individuals to become motivated self-directed learners. When students interact with one another and learn how to solve real world problems that have significance to them, they become excited about coming to school every day. Educators, and in some cases entire schools, are attempting to change students' attitudes by engaging them in these approaches to learning.

All five approaches have significant bodies of literature, and some even have professional organizations that host conferences and workshops to help educators integrate these techniques into their schools and classrooms. The amount of literature in these areas continues to increase and there appears to be a growing movement to use teaching methods that promote active participation in the classroom. Pulling these approaches together may help increase awareness and lend support for their use.

These approaches are guided by certain principles, which include *promoting hands-on learning, using a problem solving process, addressing real world problems, encouraging student interaction with each other and the content, engaging in direct experience, and using multiple subjects to enhance interdisciplinary learning.* These principles are integral to experiential learning and are found in different proportions in the five teaching approaches.

For instance, project-based learning has a strong hands-on component because students are producing products with their hands. With this teaching approach students might build a birdhouse, design a web page, or create a learning portfolio, which all require using one's hands. Problem based learning on the other hand, focuses on having students undergo a problem solving process. With this approach a group of students might be asked to figure out the kilowatt hours needed to light a classroom for an hour, in which case they will need to figure out what a kilowatt is, how much energy a light bulb uses in an hour, and how many light bulbs are in the room. Some of these approaches may rely heavily on one concept, whereas others may rely on a combination. Using teaching approaches that promote experiential learning is challenging but rewarding, especially when students become motivated self-directed learners.

BRIEF HISTORY OF EXPERIENTIAL LEARNING

One would be remiss without mentioning John Dewey's contributions to the theory and practice of experiential learning. He wrote numerous books and articles that discuss the value of experience in the educational process, and is probably referenced more often in experiential learning literature than any other writer. Interestingly, he never used the term "experiential learning" in any of the titles of his articles or books, but he did discuss the intricate process of an educational experience which has provided experiential educators with a solid theoretical foundation.

John J. McDermott (1973) edited a large collection of Dewey's significant writings in a book titled *The Philosophy of John Dewey*. One of the chapters in this book is titled "The Pattern of Inquiry," and it is in this chapter that Dewey lays out his foundational principles to his learning theory that explains why he believes this theory is the "common structure" (p. 224) of learning.

He discusses a learning process that is initiated by an indeterminate situation, which is a question or problem. This starting point in the pattern of inquiry is perplexity, which is followed by observations of the facts, the development of a hypothesis or plan, and testing the hypothesis for validity (p. 230–33).

This process according to Dewey is "serial" (p. 234) not linear and reflection may occur throughout this process as one attempts to solve a problem, "the new order of facts suggests a modified idea (or hypothesis) which occasions new observations whose result again determines a new order of facts, and so on until the existing order is both unified and complete" (p. 234).

Dewey's pattern of inquiry consists of six steps; however, his explanation of this theory is very similar to the scientific method (as cited in McDermott, 1973, pp. 101–19). He explains that a relevant problem (step one) causes perplexity and desire to find an answer, which is then followed by creating a plan (step two), testing the plan against reality (step three), and reflecting on its worth (step four). The planning and testing phases of this process are what make learning active. Responding to instructor questions and reciting back information allow students to talk, but learning becomes experiential when they create plans to solve problems and test them against reality. Creating a web site, building a learning portfolio, performing a chemistry experiment, creating a piece of artwork, or building something off a blueprint, all require students to plan and test ideas in order to determine their worth. For Dewey learning requires doing something with the subject matter aside from reciting and memorizing information.

Dewey (1938a) believed this was the common structure of learning used by human beings long before formal education was introduced into society. He identifies two modes of inquiry called *common sense* and *scientific inquiry*, and both use the same learning process but for different purposes. The first would be used to solve the problems humans face with ordinary life experience, and the latter would be used to solve problems in the sciences. In either case the process is the same and people use either mode of inquiry intuitively to solve problems on a daily basis in order to sustain and maintain life. Whether building a bird house or building a space shuttle, people use this trial and error process to refine and improve upon their ideas and practices.

Experiential educators adopted this learning theory because it requires direct experience with the subject matter. When students are not allowed to test out their ideas the "subject matter becomes arbitrary, aloof—what is called 'abstract' when that word is used in a bad sense to designate something which exclusively occupies a realm of its own without contact with the things of ordinary experience" (Dewey, as cited in McDermott, 1973, p. 255). Students need to experience things firsthand by creating, designing, building, and testing ideas in order to determine their worth. Experiential learning requires learners to undergo Dewey's pattern of inquiry and test out their ideas against reality, which helps them become more effective problem solvers. Memorizing a particular method of teaching is quite different than actually applying the method in a real classroom.

The beginning of the industrial era in the United States created significant change in the delivery of education. Information grew rapidly during this time period and there was a need to formalize education so that this information could be disseminated more efficiently. The National Education Association created the committee of ten in 1893, consisting of leading scholars and educators to develop a standardized curriculum consisting of specific subject matters that were to be taught using the Carnegie unit consisting of a number of class periods, typically fifty minutes in length, throughout a semester or school year (Shedd, 2003).

This new system of education created a situation where teachers had to rely heavily on the lecture format so they could provide students with large amounts of information in short amounts of time. The onset of formal education pulled teachers away from using approaches that encouraged problem solving, and instead learning became more cerebral requiring less hands-on interaction with the subject matter.

Dewey's learning theory, which requires more time and flexibility, was not as efficient as the lecture format in disseminating large amounts of information quickly, so the pattern of inquiry gave way to information assimilation where intelligence was measured by how much students could remember, as opposed to how much they could apply. Textbooks became the primary source of information and teachers became the conduits through which this information flowed.

Dewey argued vehemently against this approach to education and believed that traditional education stifled student creativity and motivation and led to apathy and boredom. "Why is it, in spite of the fact that teaching by pouring in, learning by a passive absorption, are universally condemned, that they are still so entrenched in practice? That education is not an affair of 'telling' and being told, but an active and constructive process, is a principle almost as generally violated in practice as conceded in theory (Dewey, 1938b, p. 38). Unfortunately, passive methods of learning continue to be fairly prevalent today.

More recently in the 1970s and 1980s, individuals such as Chickering (1977), Hutchings and Wutzdorff (1988), Keeton (1976), Kolb (1984), Kraft and Sakofs (1984), and Warner-Weil and McGill (1989) authored or edited books identifying experiential learning as a learning theory that promotes active methods of learning, intentionally used by educators to enhance learning outcomes. These writers were primarily associated with the fields of adult education and outdoor education. This was in part due to two reasons. One was the *Journal of Experiential Education*, which published articles discussing the theory of experiential learning and its applications to different educational settings. A second reason stemmed from the notion that experiential learning was unique to adult learners, and articles from the adult education field identified this learning theory as foundational to the way in which adults learn best.

In addition, two professional organizations from the fields of adult education and outdoor education were created in the early 1970s that hosted regional and national conferences. The National Society of Experiential Education (NSEE) and the Association for Experiential Education (AEE) encouraged and promoted these early writings and continue today to educate individuals on the use of experiential learning in both formal and nontraditional educational settings. These early books and organizations helped create a burgeoning growth in the use of experiential learning in many educational disciplines.

Today, experiential learning has gained a foothold in a number of different fields. A recent ERIC search revealed thirty peer reviewed journal articles over the past five years that contained experiential learning in the title, none of which were about outdoor or adult education. Topics ranged from shark research to English as a second language, and the fields in which these articles were published included science, psychology, geography, counseling, industry, business, communication, and agriculture. Experiential learning has trickled into many different fields and is becoming recognized by educators as being more effective than passive methods of learning.

Writers, including the ones mentioned in the ERIC search above, continue to view experiential learning primarily in one of two ways: either as a learning process with distinct steps that one goes through to learn something, or as a direct experience occurring outside the classroom in real world settings. In *Using Experiential Learning in the Classroom*, Wurdinger (2005) argues that experiential learning is first and foremost a learning process, and secondly, that it may occur outside the classroom. Educators that view experiential learning as a process understand that students do not need to leave the classroom to learn experientially.

Working together in small groups to solve a problem, designing and completing projects, or giving formal presentations to classmates in classroom settings all entail going through a process of creating a plan, testing it to determine if it is valid, and reflecting on the process. Educators should concentrate on engaging students in a problem solving process, no matter where it occurs, because it is a vital life skill that students should acquire by the time they graduate from high school.

Educators that view experiential learning as experience occurring outside the classroom sometimes view it as something that happens spontaneously or unintentional and is unaided by an educator. This view of experiential learning suggests that learning occurs only after reflection, which is a reactive model of learning left to chance. Without guidance, the experience could result in a noneducative experience.

To be proactive, educators need to be intentional with their teaching approaches and create structures that incorporate experience with reflection in education settings. The five teaching approaches discussed in this book intentionally attempt to implement experiential learning where students undergo a problem solving process, which begins with a problem and ends with a solution. Solving the problem may entail going outside the classroom and working with any number of individuals inside and/or outside one's community.

GENERAL CONSIDERATIONS
BEFORE USING THESE APPROACHES

"You mean I can really do this for credit?" is a common reaction from students when we approve their project proposals for credit. These statements come from graduate students who are professionals in their own fields planning projects that have practical relevancy to their work environments. They are usually surprised to discover that they are free to create and implement a project they can use in their work place. Interestingly, when given the freedom, they often do projects that entail more work than the required credit hours.

Their reactions give us the impression that their own educational experiences did not provide them with the freedom needed to pursue self-directed learning. The educational system seems to promote an environment where teachers control what and how the students learn. We are not implying that most educators are classroom dictators; however, the system appears to promote certain values like control and discipline. It penalizes students for making mistakes and so an atmosphere of secrecy and competition is promoted. We need to value mistakes because that is how people learn. We also need to give students more freedom to pursue the learning that they feel is important and relevant to their lives so that they are motivated and excited about learning.

Imagine if you were totally free to do whatever you wanted in your classroom or learning environment. Imagine teaching without any confines—no mandated tests, no mandated assessment procedures, and no mandated system wide rules to follow. You could use any materials and methods, and concentrate on one thing: student learning. What would you do? What would you use for materials and how would you create an exciting learning environment where students couldn't wait to get to class?

The teaching approaches discussed in this book do not promote values like secrecy and competition; they promote excitement and critical thinking. With these approaches teachers take a less visible role in the classroom. Educators using these approaches guide students through the learning process and encourage them to help each other solve problems and learn from making mistakes. Students are given more freedom to undergo the learning process and educators help them when they get stuck so they can keep moving forward with their own learning. Educators are not the center of attention in the classroom, student learning is.

A different type of classroom culture needs to be created when using these teaching approaches. For instance, the role of the teacher is to guide students in designing meaningful learning experiences and allowing them time to complete and present them to their peers. Students become active participants with these teaching approaches and need to understand that a different culture will unfold. Issues such as the teacher's role, the student's role, time frames, and presentation formats, should be discussed and explained. Below is a list of concepts you might want to discuss with your class before using these approaches:

Teacher's Role

1. The teacher will act as a guide allowing students to make mistakes and learn from them along the way.
2. Teachers will provide students with freedom to experiment in order to discover solutions to the problems they encounter.
3. The teacher will provide students with resources and information when they get stuck so that they can continue moving forward with their learning.

Student's Role

1. Students will be allowed freedom in the classroom as long as they are moving forward in the learning process.
2. Students may need to undergo a series of trials and errors as they attempt to complete the assignment.
3. Students should understand that the problem solving process becomes as important as the content being learned.

Time Frame

The time frame will be determined by your school structure. Some schools are bound to fifty-minute class periods, whereas others may have block scheduling. The amount of time needed to complete the project will depend on your school's structure. If you are bound to fifty-minute class periods you might identify a series of projects that may be completed in fifty minutes, or you might have one larger project that requires several class periods to complete. Block scheduling or labs in university settings allow students to do larger projects because they have more time to complete them. You will need to think about the amount of time you have in your curriculum to work on projects and then identify class time to work on them.

Presentations

Certain charter schools across North America that use experiential approaches rely heavily on presentations as a tool to evaluate student learning. The Metropolitan Regional Career & Technical Center, a charter high school in Providence, Rhode Island, uses presentations as an assessment tool. Littky and Grabelle (2004), who are intricately involved in this school, describe presentations as "kids getting up and talking passionately about a book they've read, a paper they've written, drawings they've made, or even what they know about auto mechanics. It is a way for students to have conversations about the things they have learned" (p. 7).

Project based charter schools such as the ones created by EdVisions, an organization that helps schools integrate project based learning, also have their students do presentations after completing their projects. They hold presentations about every six weeks where the public is invited to the school to listen to students present their projects. They also have students do a major exhibition after completing their senior projects, which usually require 300 to 400 hours of research. When students do presentations they "take their projects more seriously, they get valuable practice speaking in public, the parents better understand the learning process, the public knows the school is serious about academics, and it builds community" (Newell, 2005, p. 14).

In our graduate classes, students often complete short presentations throughout the semester and a longer presentation at the end of the semester. Typically, one significant project is due at the end of the semester with students presenting their projects within a 20- to 30-minute time frame. Even if all the presentations have to be squeezed into one class period, it provides them with the opportunity to explain to their peers what they did, how they did it, and what they learned from doing it. Keep in mind that the presentation format is less important than having them verbally explain what they learned from the experience.

Having students present their projects after they complete them helps solidify their learning and should be considered as an assignment when using these teaching approaches. Presentations help students organize their thoughts, express their ideas and opinions, and reflect on the important things they've learned during the process. Project presentations are different than many typical classroom presentations because students are speaking from direct experience and not about abstract theory, which they have no connection with. Direct experience allows them to comprehend and speak more intelligently about the subject matter because they tested their ideas in a real world setting. An exhibition helps them learn to organize their experience and put it into words that will hopefully be understood by their audience. Once again time frame is important to consider, as some classroom teachers may not be able to afford giving up several class periods in order for students to do presentations. But, short ones are better than none at all.

So, let go of some control and let students take control of their own learning. You too will make mistakes as you attempt to implement these teaching approaches that promote experiential learning. In order to continue your own professional development you need to experiment and try new things in the classroom. Let your students know up front that you might make some mistakes but that you will all move forward and continue to learn from these mistakes. You don't need to have all the correct answers all the time. That is what learning is all about—pursuing questions and problems that you don't have the answers to. Students will appreciate these approaches and will appreciate your honesty as you all move forward in discovering answers to the unknown.

Chapter Two

Active Learning

The term *active learning* is most often associated with a list of classroom strategies that include role-plays, simulations, debates, presentations, case studies, and drama. The goal of active learning is to promote student participation and interaction in the classroom. In an attempt to encourage more higher education faculty to use this approach, authors such as Barkley, Cross, and Howell Major (2004); Brookfield and Preskill (2005); Harmin (1994); and Meyers and Jones (1993) describe ways to intentionally integrate strategies that promote meaningful discussion in college classrooms.

These strategies attempt to engage students in discussion either individually, in pairs, or in small groups, and can easily be transferred into high school classroom settings. One teaching strategy it does not include is lecture, where students sit passively and listen to instructors do all the talking. Any strategy that promotes student interaction in the classroom could be considered active learning. These strategies were designed to occur in classroom settings where time is limited and can be conducted in a one- to three-hour time frame.

Bonwell and Eison provide a simple definition, stating that active learning is "anything that involves students in doing things and thinking about the things they are doing" (1991, p. 2). Meyers and Jones provide more detail in their definition: "active learning provides opportunities for students to talk and listen, read, write, and reflect as they approach course content through problem-solving exercises, informal small groups, simulations, case studies, role playing, and other activities—all of which require students to apply what they are learning" (1993, p. xi).

A more current definition can be found in Fink's (2003) book, titled *Creating Significant Learning Experiences,* and is broader in nature. Unlike the others, he describes active learning as a combination of experience and reflection. His view is more aligned with experiential learning where students may have to leave the classroom to get direct experience. Experience for Fink consists of doing things or observing others doing things, and reflection requires one to think about what was done and how it was done (p. 104). He agrees that direct experience is the best way for students to learn, but also falls back on the basic classroom strategies such as role-plays and case studies, which are conducted in classroom settings as opposed to real-world settings. Whether it's a role-play or a debate, the goal for Fink is to get students talking about the course content, and then have them reflect on how they might apply the information in real-life settings.

Most of the strategies imply that active learning is a group process, but according to Bonwell and Sutherland (1996), some strategies do not require students to work in groups. Presentations, for example, may be done individually, whereas debates and role-plays are designed for group interaction. Cooperative and collaborative learning are two methods that seem to have evolved out of active learning and use many of the same strategies. These two methods emphasize the importance of learning skills such as communication, responsibility, time management, and being a team player that occur when working in groups. Whether working alone or in groups, the classroom strategies are the same and attempt to get students talking in the classroom.

For those who have relied on lecture as their primary teaching format, this approach may appear rather risky. Using active-learning strategies requires letting go of some control in the classroom and allowing students freedom to express their ideas, which may lead to some interesting and unexpected discussions. From our experiences, there is little question that these strategies are effective because they engage students in their learning, and create environments where students explore ideas, challenge one another's ideas, and think critically about how they feel. You will see throughout this chapter there are a variety of strategies that may be used to help promote a dynamic, exciting classroom environment.

HISTORY

The literature on active learning as a defined teaching methodology is fairly new (dating from the early 1990s), but its roots can be traced back to the early writings of John Dewey (1916/1997). Dewey, one of the early proponents of active learning, wrote a significant amount of information about the role of experience in education and emphasized the notion that learning should involve an active phase: "the nature of experience can be understood only by noting that it includes an active and a passive element peculiarly combined" (1916/1997, p. 139). For Dewey, learning requires that students take an active role by testing ideas against reality. His writings in the early 1900s provided a theoretical foundation for active learning, and today active learning has become synonymous with specific strategies such as debates and role-plays that intentionally involve students in the learning process.

Active-learning strategies are not new to classroom educators, especially high school teachers. One of the authors remembers a high school teacher back in the mid-1970s using a debate format to teach a course on environmental education. The teacher would split the class in half and have students debate environmental issues on topics such as energy use, biohazardous waste, and hunting and fishing regulations. This was the only high school class that the author remembers much about because it was interactive and provided lively discussions during every class period, unlike the rest of his classes, which consisted of the lecture format.

Even though active-learning strategies have been used for some time, it wasn't until Bonwell and Eison (1991) came out with their book, *Active Learning: Creating Excitement in the Classroom,* that the literature on this topic began to grow. This was a groundbreaking book that not only identified specific strategies, but also explained how to use them in classroom settings.

The book also pulled together important research that validated the effectiveness of active learning in improving student learning. The strategies and supporting research discussed in *Active Learning* are directed at higher education where there was at the time, and may still be, an overemphasis on passive methods of learning such as lecturing. Their book was the beginning to what is now a fairly large body of literature on active learning.

Meyers and Jones (1993) followed with a comprehensive book, titled *Promoting Active Learning: Strategies for the College Classroom.* Their book focuses on how to use active learning in higher education settings and discusses strategies such as small-group discussion, cooperative projects, simulations, role-plays, and case studies. The strategies are similar to the ones described by Bonwell and Eison, but are discussed in terms of how to use them in college classrooms.

Harmin (1994) followed a year later with her book, titled *Inspiring Active Learning: A Handbook for Teachers.* Her book consists of numerous strategies organized in a unique fashion. She discusses specific active-learning strategies that may be used to help increase student motivation and self-confidence. She also discusses how these strategies may impact the affective, social, and intellectual sides of students. Her book takes a holistic view of the learner and attempts to use strategies that tap into all sides of a human being.

Today one can find numerous books written on this topic. While conducting a search on Amazon.com, we found books on how to use active learning with all ages, including infants all the way up to graduate students. In addition, there are books on how to use it with a variety of different subject matters, as well as a variety of different populations such as Catholic students and special education students.

Active learning has become such an effective enough technique at the collegiate level that in 2000 the journal *Active Learning in Higher Education*, published by Sage, was created as a way to share and disseminate articles focused on improving the theory and practice of active learning in higher education. The creation of a journal is historically significant because it is an indication that there are a large number of individuals using this approach who are interested in reading cutting-edge research on how to improve classroom practices. The journal also indicates a need to disseminate important research that will help move the field forward in creating a larger body of literature for practitioners. Active learning has come a long way since the early 1990s.

WHAT THE RESEARCH SAYS

There is a wealth of research documenting the effectiveness of active learning in many subjects and in many grade levels. Bransford, Brown, and Cocking (1999) found that when students are actively engaged in the learning process, they are able to not only understand more complex material, but are able to transfer their learning from one problem-solving context to another.

On the other hand, more recent studies discovered that students like lectures as much as active learning when they provide necessary test information. Machemer and Crawford (2007) and Messineo, Gaither, Bott, and Ritchey (2007) found that students prefer lectures at times because they are able to focus on collecting information that will be on their tests, which helps them achieve their desired grades. When grades, not learning *per se*, are the desired goal, then students want lectures in order to improve their grades. Students in these studies enjoyed active learning, but only if it would not affect their grades.

The Bransford, et al. (1999) study showed that active learning promotes problem-solving skills, whereas Machemer and Crawford's (2007) study suggests that memorizing information in order to receive a good grade on a test may be equally valued by students when grades are the ultimate goal. Unfortunately, the education system has created a situation where knowledge equates to memorizing information, and one's ability to solve problems seems to hold little value.

HOW TO USE ACTIVE LEARNING

Certain active-learning strategies focus more on individual involvement such as having students do presentations in front of the class, whereas other strategies are designed for small-group interaction, such as debates and role-plays. Collaborative and cooperative learning use active-learning strategies, but their primary focus is on how to effectively promote group processes while using these strategies. It is our belief that the goal of active learning is to engage students in their learning through active participation, regardless of whether they are learning individually or working in small groups. Therefore, our attention in this section focuses primarily on how to use active-learning strategies in classroom settings, as opposed to how to organize and manage group processes.

There are a number of resources that describe in detail how to design and implement discussion strategies, role-plays, debates, simulations, case studies, and drama (see the Resources section of this chapter), so instead of repeating this information, we will provide strategies that we have used in our own classes for numerous years; we know from experience that they work. Some of our strategies are very similar to those found in other books, but we describe them in a different way, according to how we used them in our own courses. In addition to providing these strategies, we discuss ways to involve students with instruction and curriculum, such as teaching short sections of the class and choosing reading materials for class discussion.

Many educators have probably experienced the difficulty in getting students to discuss ideas in their classes. Students in our classes have told us stories of when they tried to generate discussions with their own students, but had little or no success. Why is it so difficult to get students talking in class? Unfortunately, trying to jump-start a discussion is challenging when reading materials and questions don't resonate with learners. We wonder how many educators over the years have attempted to implement active learning, but reverted back to lecturing because it was familiar and less risky than trying to generate discussions?

Both process and content must be considered when attempting to engage students in meaningful discussions. With active learning, we define *process* as a class format consisting of presentations and discussions occurring between individual students and the whole class, which includes the instructor; and between students and other students. *Content* refers to reading materials and multimedia such as videos and PowerPoint presentations. In order to generate discussions, the content and questions about the content must be relevant.

According to Strong, Silver, and Perini, content that is rigorous should be "organized around complex interrelated concepts, concerned with central problems in the discipline that challenge students' previous concepts, able to arouse strong feelings, and focused on symbols and images packed with multiple meanings" (2001, p. 7). When using this type of content, discussions are easier to generate. Traditional textbooks typically do not provide this type of content and are usually filled with facts and figures that are indisputable, having very little, if any, emotional connection to students. Strong et al.'s list of principles that promote rigor suggests that educators may need to use books that challenge status quo assumptions and raise questions about the validity of the information in those books.

Professors in higher education have more academic freedom than high school teachers and can choose reading materials that cause students to question commonly held assumptions. Public school teachers may find it difficult to change their reading materials because textbooks are often aligned with meeting curriculum standards; however, good textbooks often have a list of chapter questions that may help initiate discussions. In addition, educators can develop their own chapter questions that challenge commonly held views found in these textbooks.

The authors of this book use two types of questions that help learners understand the content and connect it to their own lives We use a combination of what we call *content questions* and *personal experience questions.* Content questions are about the reading material and ask students to express their level of understanding of the material. Personal experience questions ask students to talk about an experience that somehow relates to the reading material, and to explain how the experience connects to the content.

Along with using these types of questions, we use a variety of strategies that get students talking in class. Following are a few strategies that we have tested in our classrooms using these types of questions and know from experience that they work.

Daily Presentations

A daily presentation requires each student in the class to give a short presentation on the reading material to the large group. Depending on the length of the class period, presentations could be as short as thirty seconds or as long as five minutes. We usually have students do a two- to three-minute presentation in our graduate seminars. With larger class sizes, the instructor may choose to have half the class do daily presentations during one class period, and the other half do presentations during the next class period. With a little creativity, daily presentations could even be incorporated into large lecture classes by breaking the class into small groups and having students do daily presentations within their small groups simultaneously.

Daily presentations in our classes have three different formats. One format is to provide a summary of the reading. Summaries may be partial in that the presenter may choose to summarize only a certain section of the reading because it was the section he or she could relate to the most. Or, the presenter may summarize the entire reading. The purpose of the second format is to take issue with the reading. For instance, students might argue against the ideas presented in the reading and explain why they think the author's ideas are incorrect. The third format is to relate a personal experience to the reading and explain how the experience is connected to reading.

Guidelines for Daily Presentations

- Everyone in the designated group gives a presentation. (The group could be the entire class or a portion of class.)
- No interruptions or questions are allowed during these presentations. (One exception is to ask clarifying questions so that everyone understands what the presenter means. Clarifying questions may be asked by the instructor or by peers.)
- Everyone takes notes during presentations. (Notes may consist of comments and questions about presentations.)
- Questions from the group may be asked after all the presentations are completed.

Advantages of Daily Presentations

- Daily presentations help break the ice because all students have a chance to express their ideas in a nonthreatening environment, which encourages shyer students to speak up in class.
- Everyone has an opportunity to talk, which helps prevent domineering students from doing all the talking.
- Students must read the material and understand it well enough to give a presentation on it.

Disadvantages of Daily Presentations:

- Presentations may become repetitious, especially for the last few individuals, because presenters are discussing the same material.
- Daily presentations may take more time than the class period provides, depending on the number of students and length of the presentations.

Large-Group Discussion

Large-group discussion is a free-flowing discussion among the entire class and is particularly effective when used directly after daily presentations. The large-group discussion is particularly effective after daily presentations because the ideas presented are still fresh in students' minds. Often, students will have written questions that they want to ask specific individuals about their daily presentations. One question often precipitates other questions, and the discussion takes off without much prompting from the instructor. In a sense, daily presentations help springboard the entire class into a large group discussion In the event that students do not have any questions, the instructor should be prepared with a list of questions that can be asked immediately after the daily presentations. In fact, we often have a list of questions that we bring to class; however, we also write down new questions as students do their daily presentations. In some cases, we have discarded all the questions we created before class in exchange for a list of new ones we generated during class. These new questions tend to be more relevant and meaningful to students because they are specifically created from students' presentations.

Guidelines for Large-Group Discussion

- Generate a list of questions prior to class.
- Create new questions while students do their daily presentations.
- Have students generate questions during daily presentations that they would like to ask a specific student or the large group.
- Facilitate the discussion by keeping track of who is next in line to speak.
- Provide some type of closing comments to end the discussion such as a summary of the discussion.

Advantages of Large-Group Discussion

- Allows everyone to hear all the comments and questions, which provides a common experience for the entire class.
- Allows for a greater diversity of ideas to be expressed.

Disadvantages of Large-Group Discussion

- Shy people tend not to talk much in larger classes.
- Students who are not interested in the topic might "check out" and fail to participate.

Small-Group Discussion

In small-group discussions, students are broken into groups of four to six people and are responsible for discussing a question or series of questions for a predetermined amount of time. In our classes, we have the group determine who will record notes from the discussion and who will present the information discussed to the large class after the small-group discussion is over. This strategy may be used at the outset of the class period or it might follow daily presentations.

The instructor can create a different set of questions for each small group or use the same set for each group. Students often have a different set of responses to the same set of questions. Another option is to have students generate their own questions for their small groups. This may take some added time, but the discussion might be more engaging if students create questions that they are most interested in discussing. Depending on the number and depth of the questions, instructors might have students do one small-group discussion during a class period or they might have them do several. This obviously depends on the size of the class, the length of the class period, and the instructor's goals.

Guidelines for Small-Group Discussion

- Explain process, including time lines, discussion questions, identifying a recorder, and identifying a presenter.
- Give students a time limit to discuss questions and let them know when they have a few minutes left so they can begin to formulate their presentation for the large group.
- If this strategy is used multiple times during a course, the instructor should have students switch roles so others have a chance to record notes and present.
- Have students present to the large group and, if time permits, allow for follow-up questions.
- End class with a summary of responses.

Advantages of Small-Group Discussion

- Allows students to get to know other students in the class.
- Allows students more in-depth time to discuss questions.
- Easier for shy students to talk in small groups.

Disadvantages of Small-Group Discussion

- Instructor has less control over what is being discussed in small groups.
- Groups may get off track.
- Some students might not participate.

Teaching Episode

In a teaching episode, students teach a portion of a class period or an entire class period. When students do teaching episodes in our classes we often have them design a lesson plan that they use to stay organized and on track when teaching the class. Teaching episodes may be done individually or in small groups. We prefer individual teaching episodes if possible, because this immerses students into the full experience of teaching; however, smaller groups of two or three are also used, providing that all students have opportunities to teach a section of the lesson. Organizing a larger group for a teaching episode is challenging when trying to provide equal amounts of teaching time for each group member.

The length of the episode depends on a variety of factors such as the age of the student, size of the class, and length of the period. Shorter episodes of five to ten minutes might be more effective for high school students, whereas graduate students may prefer one to two hours. Designing a lesson for the first time and teaching it to peers is challenging for students who have never taught before, so instructors might want to begin with shorter episodes at the beginning of a course and end with longer ones.

Instructors might have to use the small-group approach with larger classes, especially when time is an issue. Using small groups of four or five, for example, can still be effective, but may require more guidance from the instructor. A group of five students, for example, could do a ten-minute episode with each student having two minutes of actual teaching time. The instructor may have to help students in this situation organize the lesson so that there are five two-minute episodes back to back.

In addition, instructors can arrange larger classes, such as those found in lecture halls, into groups of five or ten and have students do individual teaching episodes within these groups. Even with larger classes, instructors can find ways to arrange them so that students have opportunities to experience teaching episodes.

Guidelines For Teaching Episodes

- Provide students with a specific amount of time for the teaching episode.
- Have students write some sort of lesson plan that will help keep them organized and on track.
- Have students practice the teaching episode before doing it with the class.
- If possible, provide students with technology such as a PowerPoint projector, an overhead, and Internet access.

Advantages of Teaching Episodes

- Helps solidify the learning when students teach the material.
- Allows students opportunities to plan a lesson, teach it, and reflect on how well they did.

Disadvantages of Teaching Episodes

- More challenging to use this strategy with large groups.
- Challenging to provide equal teaching time for each student when working in groups.

Peer Critiques

In peer critiques, students create a product such as a piece of writing, a presentation, a document, a construction project, a piece of art work, or a portfolio, and share it with a peer for critique. The length of the critique often depends on the product and guidelines to be used for the critique. In our classes, critiques often require twenty to thirty minutes. We have students pair up and review each other's work, and then one student at a time provides the other with verbal feedback on the assignment. Critique guidelines are specific to the assignment and help keep students focused on the content, which helps prevent them from feeling that they are being attacked on a personal level.

We primarily use this strategy with our students for writing and presentation assignments. Students write a short paper or create a short presentation and bring them to class for critique. Prior to the critique, we provide students with a list of guidelines. For example, with writing assignments we suggest that the critique focus on clarity, flow, sentence structure, and grammar, whereas with presentations we have critiques focus on length, voice tone, and speaking about the topic as opposed to reading it verbatim. Peer critiques help students revise and refine their papers and presentations prior to presenting them to the entire class.

Guidelines for Peer Critiques

- Provide students with a list of guidelines for critiquing each other's work.
- Provide time lines and process for the critique.
- Provide ample time for them to do an adequate job of critiquing each other's work (the process often takes longer than one would expect).
- Provide time for students to refine their assignments after the critique.
- Provide opportunities for students to present papers and presentations to the large class if time permits.

Advantages to Peer Critiques

- Allows students the opportunity to learn how to conduct a professional critique.
- Is more efficient than having the instructor critique large numbers of assignments.

Disadvantages of Peer Critiques

- Critiques may not be as thorough as those provided by the instructor.
- Might be viewed by students as doing some of the instructor's work.

MAXIMIZING THE LEARNING

Creating a psychologically safe learning environment is important when using active-learning strategies because it allows students to express their ideas without fear of being ridiculed. This is a challenging task. One way to do this is for students, along with educators, to discuss past educational experiences where they have felt insecure. *Cultural suicide* and *impostorship* (Brookfield, 2006, p. 76–84) are two types of experiences that individuals often undergo while involved in academic endeavors, but are rarely discussed in classroom settings. Discussing these types of experiences at the outset of a course may help foster a more open learning environment where students feel safe when expressing their ideas to their peers.

Cultural suicide is a phenomenon that occurs when individuals, particularly college students, learn new things, but feel alienated from friends and peers when expressing their excitement about their new learnings. Students exposed to exciting educational experiences are often enthused about telling others; unfortunately, friends may not be so enthused to receive this information. Friends may feel that they are being talked down to and may become disinterested because they are not able to relate to these educational experiences.

In some cases the student might choose to keep silent, which squelches the learning process. This phenomenon happens to many college students, and discussing this topic in class might help students realize that there are others in the class who have experienced the same thing. Discussing cultural suicide could be a uniting experience for many students in a class, helping to foster an open learning environment where students feel safe when expressing their ideas.

Impostorship occurs when learners feel they are not as smart as their peers and are impostors in an environment where they do not belong. Everyone around them appears smarter and more articulate, which creates feelings of insecurity and doubt about one's own intellectual capabilities. Both educators and students experience this phenomenon, and discussing this topic openly in class may help create a more authentic and real learning environment, which eases the fear of appearing less intellectual when talking in class.

Holding discussions on these two topics seems to even the playing field and helps students realize that they all have had similar experiences. Our own experiences with using these topics for discussion in our classes have been very favorable. Students seem to be more relaxed after discussing insecurities and appear more eager to talk in class. Discussing these topics at the outset of a course is especially effective because it helps lay the foundation for a safe learning environment. Furthermore, it seems that when these topics are discussed at the outset, students continue to grow in confidence throughout the semester and become more articulate when expressing their ideas.

RESOURCES

Website Resources

Active Learning, University of Oklahoma Instructional Development Program: http://honolulu.hawaii.edu/intranet/committees/FacDevCom/guidebk/teachtip/active.htm

Active Learning Centre Homepage test database: http://www.med.jhu.edu/med center/quiz/home.cgi

Active Learning on the Web, Department of Educational Technology, San Diego State University: http://edweb.sdsu.edu/people/bdodge/active/Active Learning.html

The Active Learning Site Homepage, Charles Bonwell: http://www.active-learning-site.com/work1.htm

Center for Teaching, Learning, and Technology, Illinois State University: http://www.cat.ilstu.edu/additional/tips/newActive.php

Print Resources

Active Learning in Higher Education: This journal's objective is to improve teaching and learning as professional activity and embraces academic practice across all curriculum areas in higher education.

Innovations in Education and Teaching International: This journal focuses on providing practitioners and decision makers with information about the developments in education, teaching, and learning.

Journal of Classroom Interaction: A refereed journal that publishes articles on the domain of classroom interactions, with special emphasis on innovative teaching and learning.

Journal of Teaching and Learning: Refereed journal that publishes a variety of topics, with special emphasis on innovative practices in teaching and learning.

NSEE Quarterly: Quarterly publication of the National Society for Experiential Education, an association of educators, businesses, and community leaders.

Chapter Three

Problem-Based and Inquiry-Based Learning

Finding solutions to authentic problems through in-depth investigation is the essence of *problem-based learning*. In so doing, it provides opportunities for learners to work collaboratively, use their informal and formal prior knowledge, engage in constructivism, and develop their self-directed learning skills (Schmidt, Loyens, Van Gog, & Paas, 2007, p. 92). Problem solving and inquiry also help learners to develop observation and reasoning skills (Inquiry Learning Forum, 2008). The Problem-Based Learning Network (2008, n.p.) offers this description of the instructional method:

> Problem-based learning is an educational approach that organizes curriculum and instruction around carefully crafted "ill-structured" problems. Students gather and apply knowledge from multiple disciplines in their quest for solutions. Guided by teachers acting as cognitive coaches, they develop critical thinking, problem solving, and collaborative skills as they identify problems, formulate hypotheses, conduct data searches, perform experiments, formulate solutions and determine the best "fit" of solutions to the conditions of the problem.

Definitely, curricula that are derived from the learner's world, rather than predetermined by the educator or educational system, stems from differing paradigms of knowledge construction. A comparison list from the Problem-Based Learning Network (2008) reveals some of the core educational beliefs held by educators who use problem-based learning and other experience-based approaches (Table 3.1). When curriculum is viewed as deriving from the experience of the learner, coherence and relevance increase, there is more whole-to-part reasoning, and learning is viewed as constructing rather than as receiving.

Table 3.1.   Curriculum as Prescription Versus Experience

Curriculum as Prescription	Curriculum as Experience
From the Perspective of the Teacher/Expert	From the Perspective of the Student/Learner
Linear and rational	Coherent and relevant
Part-to-whole organization	Whole-to-part organization
Teaching as transmitting	Teaching as facilitating
Learning as receiving	Learning as constructing
Structured environment	Flexible environment

Source: Problem-Based Learning Network, 2008.

A similar approach to problem-based learning, but one with a distinctively different historical path, is *inquiry-based learning.* Some scholars have described problem-based learning as presenting learners with a specific problem to solve and inquiry-based learning as allowing learners to determine their own problems to solve or questions to answer (Igo, Moore, Ramsey, & Ricketts, 2008). Another differentiation made by Igo et al. is that problem-based learning has a set of procedural stages, whereas inquiry learning allows the students to determine their own investigative processes. Other proponents of these approaches would disagree; for example, Hmelo-Silver, Duncan, and Chinn (2007) claim that the usage of problem-based and inquiry-based learning is, today, indistinguishable and is only in need of differentiation when discussing their historical foundations.

Whether these two approaches are the same or different will not be solved in this chapter. However, it is acknowledged that they share extensive commonalities. Therefore, to move past the argument and examine both approaches simultaneously, this chapter combines the two terms and refers to them as *PL/IL* when discussing them as they are implemented today, and by their separate names when that is more appropriate for the discussion at hand. To begin, an historical perspective on the origin of the two approaches is presented in the following section.

HISTORY

Humans have naturally engaged in problem-solving and inquiry-seeking activities since the beginning of their existence. Acknowledging that, it can be accurately stated that educational philosopher, John Dewey, was a pioneer in articulating problem-based and inquiry-based learning as intentional educational approaches (Hmelo-Silver, 2004), although he did not use those specific terms. One noteworthy contribution Dewey made to PL/IL was his *pattern of inquiry,* a set of procedures for investigating and solving problems, also referred to by him as *indeterminate situations* (as cited in McDermott, 1981, p. 227). Dewey described *inquiry* as the controlled transformation of an indeterminate situation into a determinate one whose elements are brought together into a unified whole (McDermott, 1981, p. 227). His pattern of inquiry, perhaps more commonly known as *the scientific method,* forms the basis of what is used by researchers and young learners alike to solve problems, needs, and difficulties every day. To briefly recap from chapter 1, the basic steps of the pattern of inquiry are the following: (1) identify the problem, (2) make a plan for solving the problem, (3) form a hypothesis, (4) test the planned solution, (5) assess or reflect on the solution, and (6) make a new plan if the solution did not work or apply the successful solution to a new situation or new problem (Dewey, 1938a).

As previously ascertained, the ways that problem-based and inquiry-based learning are used today are so similar that the terms can be and often are used interchangeably. Because they do possess different historical roots, however, they will be addressed separately in the following paragraphs.

Problem-Based Learning

During the 1960s, medical educators were formulating opinions that the usual programs of study based on lectures and intensive clinical sessions were not adequately or humanely preparing their students for medical practice (Savery, 2006). The traditional programs also did not allow for opportunities to use "hypothetical deductive reasoning" (p. 10) or to use context to aid students in applying what they learned. Medical knowledge had grown to the point where memorization and retrieval was challenging and exhaustive. In response, McMaster University Medical School (2008) in Ontario began to focus parts of its training programs on solving actual problems of medical practice by combining "small group, cooperative, self-directed, interdependent, self-assessed" (n.p.) learning approaches. These approaches also altered the role of the instructor from lecturer and examiner to facilitator and tutor. The Medical School began to refer to this combined approach as simply *problem-based learning,* and is recognized as the originator of the term. The approach soon spread throughout the medical field in North America and Europe, and was soon adopted and morphed by various other disciplines and grade levels (Savery, 2006). Resources, publications, and curricular materials on problem-based learning can be found today in psychology, business, education, law, social work, and engineering (Schmidt et al., 2007), and economics, architecture, and teacher education (Savery, 2006).

A website sponsored by McMaster University (2008) points out that educators often incorrectly refer to any approach that focuses on problem-solving as *problem-based learning,* which may or may not include the specific aspects quoted previously that have been shown to improve student learning. In response, today, the approach is described on the website as "small group, self-directed, self-assessed problem-based learning" (n.p.) to differentiate it from other forms.

Inquiry-Based Learning

Learning through inquiry is "a dynamic approach to learning that involves exploring the world, asking questions, making discoveries, and rigorously testing those discoveries in the search for new understanding" (Inquiry Learning Forum, 2008, n.p.). Inquiry-based learning also emerged during the 1960s, but is not attributed to any particular person or institution. It was an outgrowth of the discovery learning movement during that time, which was reacting against traditional memorization teaching methods. Discovery learning was shaped by cognitive psychologist Jerome Bruner, who advocated heavily for elements of self-directed learning (Kirschner, Sweller, & Clark, 2006). The use of pure discovery learning, where students receive little or no instructor guidance, has lessened since its inception as new insights have been gained on how the brain learns and stores knowledge.

Inquiry-based learning stemmed from K–12 classroom settings, and therefore was not focused on solving problems of professional practice in a given field, as was the case in problem-based learning. Instead, inquiry was centered on authentic, real-life problems in contexts that would help students learn concepts derived from the classroom curriculum (Exploratorium Institute for Inquiry, 2008a).

Problem-based learning in the medical field was also traditionally theory-based and relied on hypothetical deductive reasoning to arrive at solutions. That is, medical students did not diagnose or carry out their proposed treatments on actual patients. In inquiry-based learning, scientific inquiry procedures (aka *the pattern of inquiry*) were used whereby learners often carried out and tested the plans they created to solve their problems or answer their questions (Hmelo-Silver et al., 2007). There are still proponents who ascertain that problem-based and inquiry-based methods are separate approaches. However, in actual practice, characteristics of both methods are regularly integrated and interchanged.

WHAT THE RESEARCH SAYS

Many scholarly articles on the topic of PL/IL emphasize two important meta-analyses on its effectiveness for increasing student learning. Both of these were published in 1993 in the journal *Academic Medicine*—one by Albanese and Mitchell, the other by Vernon and Blake. Both studies revealed mixed results on PL/IL outcomes, revealing admirable results for PL/IL when particular components were used and inferior results when they weren't. An additional reason for the disparity stemmed from studies with low sample sizes or with questionable research procedures (as discussed in Savery, 2006; Svinicki, 2007). In studies on the preparation of medical students, the Vernon and Blake review concluded that the use of PL/IL approaches resulted in students who were more capable in utilizing clinical knowledge, but performed lower in knowledge of basic science than their more traditionally educated peers (Svinicki, p. 102).

A more recent meta-analysis was coordinated by Newman in 2003 for the Campbell Collaboration Systematic Review Group on the Effectiveness of Problem-Based Learning, United Kingdom. Similar to the earlier reviews from 1993, Newman and associates found some studies that favored specific PL/IL methods and some that favored the non-PL/IL control or comparison groups. The main conclusion drawn by Newman, however, was that there was a great lack of clarity in research reports published on PL/IL approaches. Of the ninety-one studies collected, only twelve provided enough data to be included in their final analysis. The main informational pieces that were missing or obscure were detailed descriptions of the instructional interventions used, therefore preventing determination of what aspects of PL/IL were most effective. Newman recommended that publications more carefully scrutinize the articles they accept pertaining to PL/IL so that future effectiveness of these instructional methods can be established.

Believers on both sides of the issue of PL/IL outcomes do concur on some important points pertaining to its instructional effectiveness:

1. *Learning is increased when self-directed learning includes guidance and structure provided by instructors or facilitators.* Learners determine the agenda and direction of their problem-solving processes within predetermined parameters. During the PL/IL process, instructors are highly interactive and attuned to the progress of the individual learners or learning groups. Adjustments in instruction are made along the way that may entail scaffolding and fading activities (see item 3, following), changes in timeframes or scope, or even providing direct instruction, sometimes delivered on a "just-in-time" basis (Hmelo-Smith et al., 2007, p. 100) when learners reach a critical juncture in their knowledge base.

2. *Learning is increased when problem-solving processes are used prior to new content information being presented by the instructor or provided through other means.* The problem to be solved provides the hook (or

context) upon which the new information can be hung. A specific example discussed by Schmidt et al. (2007) involved a study with fourteen-year-old students who studied osmosis in cells first, then engaged in a problem-based learning exercise to determine the phenomenon that happened when cells were placed in salted and unsalted solutions. In a comparison group, students with limited knowledge about osmosis had a higher learning gain when the problem-based experience preceded new information on osmosis provided through instruction. The problem-based learning approach increased "the interaction between knowledge already available in the learners and the new to-be-learned information; elaboration by explanations during group discussions stimulate[d] the integration of new information into the knowledge base already present in long-term memory" (p. 93).

3. *Learning is increased when the instructors or facilitators use intentional scaffolding.* Scaffolding encompasses the various ways that instructors or tutors help learners categorize and store information into long-term memory, such as task structuring, modeling, coaching, hinting, probing, paraphrasing, and redirecting (Hmelo-Smith et al., 2007). Information introduced to learners in their working memory, which is quite limited in capacity, transfers into long-term memory when the brain is able to place it within preexisting schema. When working memory is overtaxed, resulting in what is called *cognitive load* (Sweller, 2004), the ability to retrieve or store knowledge in long-term memory is disrupted. Learners working on problems and questions during PL/IL exercises are often presented with large amounts of new information, presenting the risk of obstructing increases in long-term memory. Scaffolding significantly reduces, and at times prevents, cognitive load (Hmelo-Smith et al., 2007; Sweller, 2004).

An important discussion on PL/IL has surfaced in recent years through an article published by Kirschner et al. (2006) pertaining to human cognition architecture, which is made up of sensory, working, and long-term memory. These research scholars asserted that "the aim of all of instruction is to alter long-term memory" (p. 77) and that any instructional strategies that do not do this are ineffective. In their controversial article, Kirschner et al. lumped PL/IL together with discovery, experiential, and constructivist learning as approaches that offer "minimal guidance" (p. 76) from instructors, and claimed that research on these approaches did not show them to alter long-term memory. In brief, the authors argued that minimal-guidance instructional approaches do not result in learning.

As can be imagined, proponents of some of these approaches responded vehemently with defensive arguments. Hmelo-Silver et al. (2007) claimed it is inaccurate to describe PL/IL as minimally guided. They agreed there might be times when minimal guidance is used because it is the best approach for the particular learning situation. There are also times when lectures, direct instruction, and extensive instructor guidance may be implemented, depending on the nature and extent of previous learner knowledge of the problems being investigated. They further claimed that Kirschner et al. (2006) cited only research that backed their point of view and failed to include other studies that showed the effectiveness of PL/IL and larger gains in student knowledge than in respective comparison groups.

For example, a recent study cited by Hmelo-Silver et al. (2007) involved over nineteen thousand middle-school science students. The student groups that used inquiry-based instructional materials revealed higher pass rates on standardized tests. The gains these students demonstrated "occurred up to a year and a half after participation in inquiry-based instruction" (p. 104), showing that long-term memory had been changed. The same study revealed the elimination of a preexisting achievement gap between girls and African American boys. Another study discussed by Hmelo-Silver et al. included over two thousand eighth grade students from ten middle schools in Maryland. Students in all of the "diversity groupings" (p. 104) of limited language, socioeconomic category, ethnicity, and gender who had participated in the inquiry-based curriculum outperformed their respective comparison groups. Although some of the studies specific to problem-based learning in medical training revealed mixed findings, Hmelo-Silver et al. concluded, "There is growing evidence from large-scale experimental and quasi-experimental studies demonstrating that inquiry-based instruction results in significant learning gains in comparison to traditional instruction" (p. 104).

Schmidt et al. (2007) also objected to the association made between PL/IL and minimally guided instruction. They also summarized several studies that found PL/IL approaches to be stronger in developing long-term cognitive structures than the more extensively directed and lecture-oriented instructional approaches that Kirschner et al. (2006) claimed are necessary for learning. Although they concurred that there are mixed findings on problem-based learning research with medical students, they stressed that one limitation is due to the high levels of cognition and skills that the students are required to already possess to be accepted into medical school. This results in "ceiling effects" (Schmidt et al., 2007, p. 96) that may limit the possibilities for large gains in knowledge or certain types of decision making. Schmidt et al. additionally stressed that problem-based learning is not so much concerned with the "direct application of knowledge" (p. 96), but more so with a "flexible application" (p. 96) that aids learners in recognizing similarities in various problems, interpreting previous knowledge, determining needs and venues for further information, and choosing appropriate and viable solutions.

It should be noted that Sweller, Kirschner, and Clark (2007) did provide a commentary to the objections made by Hmelo-Silver et al. (2007) and Schmidt et al. (2007). In their response, they reasserted their original position. They further proposed that future studies on these approaches should test only one variable at a time to ensure that the results are indisputable.

HOW TO USE PL/IL

A general series of actions for PL/IL is shown in Figure 3.1 of the problem-based learning cycle adapted from Hmelo-Silver (2004). It is helpful for demonstrating the cyclical nature of the approaches whereby solving a problem often leads to new questions. It can be seen in this figure that an aim, if not *the* aim, of PL/IL is the application of the new knowledge gained to new learning or problem situations.

The Exploratorium Institute for Inquiry (2008b) provides a more detailed three-stage process structure (Figure 3.2). Basically, the first stage encompasses all that goes into planning to solve the problem, the second stage involves investigation procedures, and the third stage entails reporting or sharing the results. Several different procedures may occur within each stage.

A user-friendly diagram (Figure 3.3) located on the Youth Learn (2008) website breaks down the steps in inquiry-based learning into useful questions that can be posed to learners throughout the process. Note that the arrows between

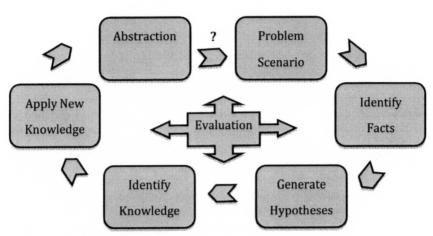

Figure 3.1. Learning Cycle for Problem-based Learning
Source: Adapted from Hmelo-Silver, 2004.

Stage 1 Inquiry Starters	Stage 2 Focused Investigation	Stage 3 Sharing Understanding
Learners explore materials, make observations and raise questions related to content goals.	Learners plan and carry out their investigations based on their questions.	Learners share investigation results with each other to further their understanding of concepts.

Figure 3.2. Three Stage Learning Cycle for Problem-based Learning
Source: Exploratorium Institute for Inquiry (2008b).

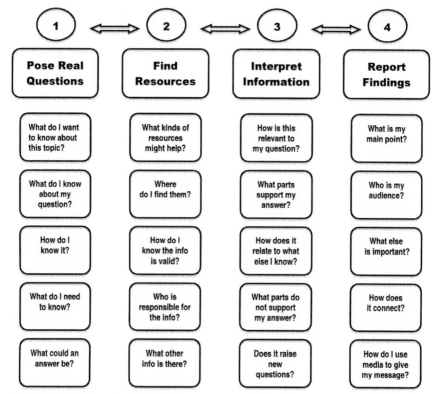

Figure 3.3. The Inquiry Process
Source: Attributed to Cornelia Brunner, Center of Children and Technology.

each of the four stages indicate a back-and-forth process whereby sometimes a bump or obstacle is encountered and requires learners to backtrack to an earlier step for reevaluation. This diagram, titled "The Inquiry Process," was attributed to Cornelia Brunner from the Center of Children and Technology. Both agencies function under the not-for-profit Education Development Center.

Concept to Classroom (2008) is an award-winning series of free, online workshops for educators that contain relevant information, resources, ideas, and video streams with real teachers in their classrooms sharing what they have learned and experienced. There is an excellent workshop available on inquiry-based learning. The idea of a facilitation plan, rather than a lesson plan, is recommended. A template is offered that contains thirteen parts, which may sound daunting at first, but is practical and realistic for facilitating all phases of PL/IL effectively. The parts are listed in Table 3.2, and are explained in more detail in the online workshop (see the Website Resources at the end of this chapter for URL address).

MAXIMIZING THE LEARNING

There are two aspects of PL/IL that appear to be especially important in maximizing learning for students. One of those has to do with *finding or creating good problems*. Two attributes of good problems are those that are complex enough to warrant in-depth investigation and those that carry enough real-life weight, so to speak, to spark and sustain student interest. White (1995) humorously stated, "[W]hen faculty consider introducing problem-based learning into their courses, one of the perceived 'problems' is a lack of suitable problems" (¶ 1). White conceded that problems provided at the end of textbook chapters often seem too narrow and inadequate for in-depth investigation. Case studies can pose intriguing, complex problems, but appropriate ones may be hard to find on the topic the instructor wants to address. Educators often, then, resort to creating their own problems, which may take a bit of time, but White noted that "once started, the activity can be enormously stimulating" (¶ 3).

White (1995) suggests mining ideas by tapping into classic works in the specific discipline, current events, everyday situations, past or current controversies, and personal experience. He claims, "the sources are almost limitless" (¶ 4). White himself has found that since first embarking on PL/IL in his chemistry classroom, he has become a constant sleuth, writing potential problems in a small notebook he carries, never knowing when or from where a good idea might surface.

Many sources on PL/IL also state that good problems are those that are "ill-structured" (Igo et al., 2008, p. 53). What this means is that there should be just enough information given to reveal a problem and stimulate learners' interests in solving it, but not enough information or structure to indicate how

Table 3.2. Inquiry-Based Learning Facilitation Plan

Aspects of Facilitation Plan	
Learning Objectives and Expected Outcomes	These may include observation skills, research skills, and synthesis skills.
Habits of Mind/Ground Rules Being Emphasized	In science, these might include aspects of the scientific method; in English, these might include literary ideals.
Conceptual Theme Most Important to This Lesson	Also might include the way the discipline explores change, or the way it makes connections between one idea and another.
Specific Content	Also might include the academic standards being sought.
Sources and Resources Needed/Available	Such as libraries, professional journals, local colleges/universities, the Internet, other professionals. Also list any materials needed.
Potential Roadblocks to Learning	Any problems students may have in learning this material. Also list possible solutions.
Inquiry Attributes Already Possessed by Learners	What are the skill levels of the learners? What habits of mind do they possess? What are their levels of conceptual understanding? Of content understanding?
Questions and Types of Questions to Be Raised and Explored	The main questions that learners might explore, as well as the various types of questions.
Ongoing Assessment	Observations, examination of student work and where they are having difficulty, records of progress.
Appropriate Sources and Resources to Effectively Monitor Progress	The ways students will be assessed at the end of the activity.
Professional Preparation	What you, as a teacher, need to find out before starting the lesson.
Long-Range, Medium-Range, and Short-Range Goals	Overall learning goals for the year, for the major units of study, and for the specific learning experience.
Plans to Help Advanced Learners Become Facilitators for Learners Needing Additional Help	Ways that advanced students can work with others as the project or projects progress.

Source: Concept to Classroom (2008).

it might be solved or what a probable solution might be. Igo et al. recommend that problems for use in PL/IL should:

1. Confuse just enough to provoke curiosity and provide a reason for learning.
2. Provoke thought on new things in new ways.
3. Help students discover what they do and do not know.

4. Ensure that students reach beyond what they know.
5. Create a need and desire for skill and knowledge.
6. Lead to understanding the relationship of a procedure to the problem that makes the procedure sensible.
7. Naturally lead to interdisciplinary inquiry.
8. Build strong communities of learners.
9. Create cooperation in the strongest sense that is based on the will and desire to succeed rather than on a set of dictated behaviors that are advocated for the sake of politeness. (p. 53)

The other aspect of PL/IL for maximizing learning pertains to *effective facilitation of the problem-solving process*. Although students are involved in self-directed learning, this does not mean that there is no teacher involvement. Quite the opposite is true—there is much more teacher-to-student interaction than lecture and other direct instruction types of teaching provide. The role of the instructor, in comparison with more traditional instructional styles, is to ask rather than tell, to pose questions rather than answer them, to probe rather than critique, to redirect rather than direct, to entice rather than push, to suggest rather than require, and to encourage self-evaluation rather than evaluate.

Another skill in facilitation is for educators to become adept at "fading" the guidance they provide (Hmelo-Smith et al., 2007). This is based on the "guidance fading effect" (Sweller, 2004, p. 25) that results when instruction is lessened as learners' knowledge increases. In practice, then, instructors of PL/IL provide more guidance or instruction when needed (when content knowledge is low, at the beginning of a new problem-solving process, or when learners are first learning how to problem-solve), and then slowly lessen their presence and the amount of instructional help they provide as learners demonstrate their growing knowledge base. The guidance fading effect is similar to what parents do when helping their children learn to ride a bicycle—they are always available and close by if needed, but are hands-off once the child can keep the momentum going.

Crafting good problems and facilitating effective problem-solving processes are not easy skills to hone. Although there are professional development workshops and specific trainings for educators offered by numerous organizations on PL/IL, one cannot become an exemplary implementer of PL/IL without practice, diligence, and reflection over time.

RESOURCES

Website Resources

Exploratorium Institute for Inquiry: http://www.exploratorium.edu/IFI/

Inquiry-Based Learning Workshop, Concept to Classroom: Free, self-paced online workshop for educators on inquiry-based learning with video streams available through Thirteen Ed Online at http://www.thirteen.org/edonline/concept2class/inquiry/index.html

Inquiry Learning Forum, Indiana University: http://ilf.crlt.indiana.edu/

Inquiry and the National Science Education Standards: A guide for teaching and learning. Full content available free online at http://books.nap.edu/html/inquiry_addendum/index.html

Maastricht University (Universiteit Maastricht) PBL-site, The Netherlands: http:/www.unimaas.nl/pbl/default.htm

Problem-Based Learning Network, Illinois Mathematics and Science Academy: http://pbln.imsa.edu/

Process Oriented Guided Inquiry Learning: http://www.pogil.org/

Print Resources

Evensen, D. H., & Hmelo-Silver, C. E. (Eds.). (2000). *Problem-based learning: A research perspective on learning interactions.* Philadelphia: Lawrence Erlbaum Associates.

Torp, L., & Sage, S. (2002). *Problems as possibilities: Problem-based learning for K–16 educators* (2nd ed.). Alexandria, VA: Association for Supervision & Curriculum Development.

Chapter Four

Project-Based Learning

Project-based learning is one approach to teaching that is motivating students and improving schools across the United States because it inspires students to learn and changes their attitudes about school (Blumenfeld, Soloway, Marx, Krajcik, Guzdial, & Palincsar, 1991; Grant & Branch, 2005; Levine, 2002; Littky & Grabelle, 2004; Newell, 2003; Thomas, Enloe, & Newell, 2005). According to Pearlman (2009), today's students need a different set of skills that include learning and thinking skills, technology literacy skills, and life skills in order to compete in the future. Pearlman argues that these skills can best be obtained through project-based learning.

At the high school level, charter schools and independent schools, which have more freedom to design their own curriculums, tend to use project-based learning more than mainstream public schools. Markham (personal communication, March 2007) estimates there are approximately two thousand schools in the United States involved in the small-schools movement that use project-based learning in one form or another. In higher education one is more likely to find individual faculty members using project-based learning. There are, however, a few degree programs that use it extensively, and in one case an entire university, Northface, uses this approach with all its degree programs.

Project-based learning is a teaching method that taps into students' interests because it allows them to create projects that result in meaningful learning experiences. Railsback has identified a number of important benefits of project-based learning: it is active not passive, it is interesting and relevant to the student, it allows for autonomy and self-directed learning, it increases communication skills, and it enhances motivation to learn (2002, p. 9). Increasingly, teachers and schools across the United States are beginning to use this method because they know it challenges students on an individual level, motivating and inspiring them through their own interests and learning styles.

Individuals who have implemented project-based learning in different educational settings have created some useful definitions. Ron Newell, co-director of EdVisions, a not-for-profit organization that has created over thirty charter schools across the nation, defines project-based learning as a process that "emphasizes student interest rather than following a fixed curriculum; emphasizes a broad, interdisciplinary focus rather than a narrow, discipline-based focus; uses direct, primary, or original sources rather than texts, lectures, and secondary sources; emphasizes data and materials developed by students rather than teachers" (2003, p. 5).

Another organization promoting the use of project-based learning is the Buck Institute for Education. This organization published the *Project Based Learning Handbook: A Guide to Standards-Focused Project Based Learning for Middle and High School Teachers* to help educators integrate project-based learning into their existing curriculums. The handbook defines project-based learning as "a systemic teaching method that engages students in learning knowledge and skills through an extended inquiry process structured around complex, authentic questions and carefully designed products and tasks" (Markham, Larmer, & Ravitz, 2003, p. 4).

Wurdinger, Haar, Hugg, and Bezon, who have helped educators implement this technique in K–12 and higher education settings, define project-based learning as "a teaching method where teachers guide students through a problem solving process which includes identifying a problem, developing a plan, testing the plan against reality, and reflecting on the plan while in the process of designing and completing a project" (2007, p. 151). This definition relies heavily on Dewey's (1938b) theory of learning, where students generate ideas, create plans, and test them against reality to determine their worth.

All these definitions place emphasis on student-centered learning, as opposed to teacher-directed learning. Students design and complete projects, many of which require solving multiple problems before they are able to complete them. Solving problems in order to complete a project takes more time than traditional methods of learning like the lecture format, because students may have to undergo multiple attempts before completing the project to their satisfaction. This is an important concept for educators to understand before attempting to implement project-based learning in their classrooms.

HISTORY

Project-based learning has been around for quite some time. Knoll (1997) wrote a comprehensive, interesting piece on the history of project-based learning that explains in great detail how it evolved and changed from both

European and U.S. influences. He discovered through his research that the project method was being used by the Massachusetts Institute of Technology engineering faculty as early as 1864.

This teaching method gained support from school administrators and teachers during this period, and by 1897 it was being used with "thousands of males and females at American high schools" (Knoll, 1997, p. 4) in carpentry, ironwork, cooking, and sewing courses. Some of the early polytechnic universities in the United States placed tremendous importance on projects and often required students to complete a major project in order to graduate.

Project-based learning almost lost its foothold just as it was gaining momentum in the early 1900s. William Kilpatrick, a student of John Dewey's and one of the early leaders of the progressive education movement, created confusion about project-based learning by suggesting that a project could be anything as long as it was initiated by the student. In his essay titled "The Project Method" Kilpatrick (1918) suggests that students do not need to be actively involved in the project and can sit passively listening to music, for example, in order to complete a project. Kilpatrick's essay was based on John Dewey's (1913) work titled *Interest and Effort in Education,* and according to Knoll (1997), Dewey disagreed with Kilpatrick's interpretation. Dewey believed that teachers are critical to the educational process and should guide students through experiences to enhance learning outcomes.

Although Dewey agreed with much of the essay, he argued against students having complete freedom over their own learning. Later Kilpatrick recanted and agreed that the educational process should not be left to the sole responsibility of the student. The disagreement had been settled and the project method continued gaining attention both in K–12 and higher education settings.

Stillman Robinson, professor of mechanical engineering at Illinois Industrial University, who lived during this same period had the correct conception of project-based learning because he required his students to not only draw blueprints of machines, but create working products off their blueprints (Knoll, 1997). He believed that projects should be created and built by students, so that they could understand their practical importance. Project-based learning has come a long way since Kilpatrick, Dewey, and Robinson's time, and continues to be used by schools and educators across the United States today.

WHAT THE RESEARCH SAYS

There is a wealth of research that supports the use of project-based learning in K–12 and higher educations settings. Project-based learning researchers have analyzed areas such as teacher acceptance, student motivation, and student achievement, and all have come to the conclusion that project-based learning is an effective teaching methodology. Several of these studies are highlighted in the following paragraphs.

Barron, Schwartz, Vye, Moore, Petrosino, Zech, and Bransford (1998) discovered that academic performance and motivation are greatly improved when using project-based learning. In their comprehensive study, they had students create blueprints of chairs and playhouses, and then present these drawings to their classmates. They measured low-, average-, and high-achieving students, and found that all three groups had significant improvements in their ability to understand difficult math concepts after using the project method. This approach to learning not only had a significant impact on their comprehension, but it also had a positive impact on their motivation. Fifty percent of the students interviewed about their experience specifically mentioned that the projects were a very important part of their school year (p. 305).

Cornell and Clark (1999) conducted an extensive study on standards-based teaching and learning for the primary purpose of moving teachers away from a teacher-directed lecture format toward a student-centered format where students are more engaged by initiating and completing projects. They found that students were more engaged when involved in project-based learning because it gave them an opportunity to work with other students while doing hands-on activities, which provided them with a more self-directed learning environment. Even lower performing students enjoyed the process because it not only gave them an opportunity to discover unique skills necessary to complete projects, but allowed them to progress at their own pace.

However, two of the paradoxes they discovered, "less teacher talk requires more teacher time" and "free-ranging self directed inquiry depends on a tight design structure" (Cornell & Clark, 1999, p. 94), indicate that even though motivation and student learning were enhanced through the project-based learning process, it requires more work for teachers when designing projects and preparing lessons. Teachers commented that the initial phase of the project-based learning process required a fair amount of planning time; however, once established, they were able to focus more on guiding students through the process.

Liu and Hsiao conducted a research study on using project-based learning with middle school students and found that it increased their "learning of design knowledge, their cognitive strategy use, and their motivation toward learning" (2002, p. 311). In this study, students assumed the roles of researcher, graphic artist, programmer, project manager, and audiovisual specialist, and worked together to complete multimedia presentations. Because students were directly involved in the process, they were able to understand and retain the information they were using while creating and designing their multimedia presentation. Liu and Hsiao's research clearly indicates that project-based learning has the potential to enhance both student motivation and performance in the classroom. These two authors sum up their research by claiming that students showed "substantial gains in their abilities to understand, use, and present geometric concepts" (p. 303).

Wurdinger et al. (2007) conducted a year-long study that looked at teacher acceptance and student engagement, and discovered that providing a one-day staff training to educate teachers on how to use project-based learning enhances and promotes teacher acceptance, which is critical to implementing and sustaining the use of this method in school settings. Middle school teachers interviewed about student engagement in this study were enthusiastic about using this method and stated that it "promotes discussion and peer teaching, enhances student ownership, increases higher order thinking and life skills, and promotes group cohesiveness" (p. 157). Some teachers used individual projects and others used group projects, but in either situation teachers supported the use of this method because they observed a high level of motivation when students were engaged with their projects. Some teachers stated that students were so engrossed with their projects that they did not notice the teacher was in the room. As noted by Fullan, "educational change depends on what teachers do and think—it's as simple and as complex as that" (2001, p. 115). Without teacher acceptance, innovative methods like project-based learning won't make it through the door of the classroom.

Barak and Dori (2005) conducted a research study with college freshman chemistry students and discovered that the project-based experimental group outperformed the control group who were exposed to traditional textbook chemistry problems. After being involved in a project requiring the construction of molecular models, the project-based group scored higher on their final exams and "enhanced their understanding of chemical concepts, theories, and molecular structures" (p. 117).

Gonzales and Nelson (2005), through interviews and discussions with teachers and students at Northface University, discovered that this university's use of project-based learning has convinced Global 1000 companies like IBM and Microsoft to create partnerships allowing students to work on enterprise projects within these organizations. This university enrolled its first cohort in 2004, and developed a curriculum based entirely on project-based learning. The university is growing rapidly, which indicates how practical and useful it is to its students.

HOW TO USE PROJECT-BASED LEARNING

Some schools and educators give students the freedom to determine what they want to create for a project and provide guidance through the project process only when necessary. In other cases educators provide students with predetermined projects and control the process from beginning to end. Project-based learning is the centerpiece of the curriculum for some high schools and universities, and with others it is used sparingly as extracurricular activities. In the former, students do all projects to complete their graduation requirements, whereas in the latter they might be used as after-school activities to promote social skills.

Projects may be highly structured, requiring detailed project proposals, learning outcomes, and exhibitions that are evaluated with performance-based rubrics, or they may be unstructured, nongraded activities. The type of project-based learning discussed in this chapter is structured and intentionally designed to be part of the curriculum; however, educators can easily modify these ideas into nongraded extracurricular activities.

Deciding What Variation to Use

Newell (2007) created five variations of project-based learning that explain how it is used in classroom settings. The variations are like a spectrum, with number one being entirely teacher-directed and number five being student-directed. Teachers control the entire process on one end and students on the other. It may be helpful for educators to determine what variation they wish to utilize, and use the corresponding guidelines as a tool to help implement project-based learning with their students.

1. Project is teacher-controlled:
   Project is part of curricular unit, text, etc.
   All students do the same thing.
   No student choice.
   Graded as part of class unit.
2. Project is teacher-controlled:
   Allows for student inquiry, choice of topic within curriculum.
   Students have to frame their own questions.
   All students have same time frame.
   Graded as part of class unit.
3. Project is set up and orchestrated by teacher:
   Project is inquiry-based, looks at "big picture"; still curriculum-based.
   Project is interdisciplinary and thematic in nature.

Students may be in cooperative groups, teaming.
Performance, product assessment is used as well as class grade.
4. Project created with teacher-student interaction:
   Project is interdisciplinary in nature, inquiry-based, authentic.
   Rubrics assess performances, critical thinking, and problem solving.
   Students may be in cooperative groups, teaming, or whole class.
   Includes place-based projects, community service, etc.
   Time frame is negotiable, but within semester, or units.
5. Project is student-driven, authentic:
   Project is teacher-facilitated with teachers providing the process.
   The "whole world" is the curriculum, with state standards guiding the work.
   Rubrics assess learning-to-learn skills, individual development, etc.
   Performance and products assessed, performances to real-world audience.
   May be individual or group projects.
   Could include place-based, community service projects.
   Nongraded, time frame negotiable.

Variation five is highly student-directed, and requires more freedom and larger blocks of time to implement, which may be impractical for educators in more traditional, mainstream education settings. Variations one and two might be more practical for educators who are new to project-based learning; these variations allow them to experiment using more control over the process and provide an easier transition to the other variations as they progress toward a more student-directed classroom.

One of the authors has two daughters who attend traditional mainstream schools. Both of these students have had several innovative teachers who have used variations one and two with great success in motivating students to learn. Project examples that their teachers have assigned included life collages, web designs for the school, producing television commercials, creating ancient Greek architecture using food products, and building small wooden boats.

As a parent, it was interesting to observe their behavior when involved in project work, as opposed to when they were doing traditional homework consisting mostly of reading and answering worksheets. They were highly motivated and excited, whether working in groups or alone to create their projects. No prompting was necessary to work on their projects after school. They would come home from school, immediately clear off the dining room table, and spread out all of their project materials. As they worked on their projects, they would lose track of time as they were working away, creating what were, in their minds, masterpieces. They were so immersed in the process that we would have to force them to stop and clear the table so we could eat dinner.

Even though variations one and two limit students' freedom in choosing their own projects, the increased level of motivation was obvious and therefore these variations were extremely effective. Newell (2003) argues, however, that variations four and five are more effective because when students choose projects based on their own passions, they have a vested interest in pursuing and completing them. Unfortunately, few teachers in traditional mainstream settings have the luxury of allowing their students to choose projects based on their own interests.

Working Alone or in Groups

After deciding which variation is most appropriate for your classroom setting, you will want to determine whether students will work alone or if they will be allowed to work together on their projects. This requires some thinking and planning on your part because there are definite advantages and disadvantages to each. For instance, if they work alone, then each student will be doing all of his or her own work to complete the project, whereas if they work together, it is possible that one or two students may end up doing most of the work.

If you choose to allow students to work together, then you may want to create some guidelines for the process. Identifying specific parts of the projects and assigning students to do these individual parts helps spread the workload more evenly. You might also want to identify specific jobs within the group, such as information collectors, interviewers, recorders, time keepers, builders, designers, and so on, so that everyone knows his or her role and expectations within the group.

If projects require larger amounts of time to complete, you may need to provide groups with benchmarks throughout the semester so they are more apt to follow this time line and complete the project when it is due. Reporting on their progress periodically also helps students stay on track, and allows them an opportunity to discuss problems they have encountered along the way.

From our own personal experience, group work is more challenging to manage; however, in this venue students could learn important social skills such as communication, trust building, and confidence that they otherwise wouldn't learn if they were working alone. Graduate students in our classes often seem to prefer working alone because they can create and design projects fashioned around their own personal interests that they are truly passionate about. Otherwise, they may compromise their own interests and end up working on someone else's project with little or no motivation.

Educators new to this approach might consider having their students work alone when trying to implement this approach for the first time because it is easier to manage and assess learning outcomes. Group work can be used once the educator becomes more familiar with the project-based process. There is a tremendous amount of information on theories and practices of designing and implementing group work, which is beyond the scope of this book. For more detailed information about creating effective group work, we recommend *Designing Group Work* by Elizabeth Cohen (1986), *Communicating in Small Groups* by Beebe and Masterson (2008), and *Effective Groups* by Cannon, Griffith, and Guthrie (2006).

Creating a Different Classroom Culture

After determining whether students will work alone or on group projects, you will need to determine what role you will play in the project process. How much control will you take over the process? There is no doubt that helping students identify manageable projects is important. Projects should be mentally challenging so that students engage in critical thought during the planning, testing, and reflecting phases, but should not be too challenging; otherwise students may get discouraged, which could bring the learning process to a sudden halt. But too much control may hinder the learning process. For example, when a teacher in a technical education classroom provides students with a hand-out explaining a step-by-step process on how to build a wooden clock and then demonstrates how to construct the clock, little, if any, problem solving is necessary. The students are not challenged in this situation because they simply copy what the teacher has demonstrated.

On the other hand, planning, testing, and reflecting become an integral part of the learning process if this same teacher explains to students that they need to build a working clock with certain materials and resources and then allows them to experiment on their own. Challenging students by providing them with opportunities for creative thought allows them to explore and determine what the best design and building process might be.

This approach also allows students to think creatively and become more self-directed learners. They are able to explore their own personal learning styles, and, when they succeed by completing their projects, it fosters a sense of self-worth because they realize that they can overcome challenges that at first appeared insurmountable. Project-based learning requires students to solve difficult problems, which may ultimately help students become more effective problem solvers and lead to a broader and more complete understanding of the subject matter.

At first, this process may be uncomfortable. When students are creating projects they need some freedom to move around the room or building, acquiring the necessary resources to do their projects. It may appear chaotic;

however, a classroom culture that allows for some freedom, along with clear expectations, is necessary when using this approach.

Project Length

Educators should also think about the length of the project. If the project is too big, students might have difficulty completing it within the required timeframe, or they might complete it just to get it done and miss out on valuable learning opportunities. Students, even at the graduate level, often choose projects that are too complex. It is critical to guide students through this first step; otherwise they may get frustrated and give up right away if the project is too overwhelming.

Markham et al. (2003) identified a number of different types of projects that may be used in a variety of subject areas. He identified seven types of projects, some of which are more specific to particular disciplines such as construction products for industrial technology courses, and others that are more general such as written products that may be used in any course (see Table 4.1).

Planning the Project

Once the project has been chosen, the next step is for students to gather information they might need to start creating their projects. To gather this information, students may need to conduct interviews, use the Internet or library resources, read articles and books, and find examples of projects similar in nature that have already been completed by others. During this phase of the project, educators may want to have students keep learning logs, which entails writing down the steps along the way and keeping a running tally of the time they spend working on their projects.

The educator's role during this portion of the project is to let the process unfold. Students may come to you when they have questions and need your assistance, but you must refrain from doing their work for them. Instead, give them the needed resources, which will allow them to discover the answers for themselves that they need in order to keep moving forward in the process.

Having students collect and save materials such as interview notes, printed material from the Internet or library, learning logs, and other information may serve as important artifacts that educators can use when assigning a grade to the student's work. Students should organize their artifacts in a way that can be turned in to the educator when the project is completed. Three-ring binders and computer files are two options that have worked well for our students. Educators may wish to provide students with binders that have labeled tabs so students know exactly what types of artifacts they will need to collect and

Table 4.1. Project Type

Written Products	Presentation Products	Technological Products	Media Products	Training Products	Planning Products	Construction Products
Research report	Speech	Computer database	Audiotape	Program	Proposal	Physical model
Interviews	Debate	Computer graphics	Slideshow	Manual	Estimate	Consumer product
Narrative	Play	Computer programs	PowerPoint	Curriculum	Bid	System model
Letter	Song/Lyric	CD-ROM	Videotape	Working model	Blueprint	Machine
Poster instrument	Musical piece	Websites	Drawing		Flow chart	Scientific
Proposal	Oral report		Painting		Timeline	Museum exhibit
Poem	Panel discussion		Sculpture			Diorama
Outline	Newscast		Collage			
Brochure	Discussion		Map			
Pamphlet	Dance		Scrapbook			
Survey	Data display/chart		Oral history			
Autobiography	Exhibition of product		Photo album			
Essay						
Book review						
Editorial						
Movie script						

Adapted from Markham et al., 2003, p. 59.

turn in at the end of the project. Too much structure may inhibit students from engaging in their own problem solving when completing a project, but younger students may need more direction with specific instructions like the binders mentioned previously.

Project Assessment

Many project-based schools tend to use three components to assess the project process: a proposal, learning artifacts, and a presentation or exhibition. To help students organize themselves, educators should provide handouts corresponding to each component of the project process. A project proposal form should be filled out by each student before he or she begins working on the projects. Two sample project proposal forms are provided in this chapter. Forms should include information such as the title of the project, the resources needed, a written plan to complete the project, how the project may be applied to real-life settings, and identification of potential learning outcomes. Educators may need to help guide students through this phase so that students identify a project that they can complete within the determined timeframe.

Educators should provide students with a list of possible artifacts they should collect while working on their projects. Artifacts you might want students to collect include learning logs, library references, websites, materials needed to build the project, and drawings of the project. A form could be designed for each of the artifacts listed previously, or a form including several artifacts could be specifically designed to match the project. An example of an artifact form follows.

The third component is assessing the project or presentation. Two individual rubrics, one for the project and the other for the presentation, can be handed out so that students know ahead of time how they will be evaluated. To help students do well, the evaluation items on the rubric should be clearly spelled out. For instance, if the project entails building something, then a project rubric might include items like design, length, weight, and function. A second rubric could be fashioned around a demonstration of the project via an oral presentation and include items like explanation of materials and design, clarity and flow of speech, and length of presentation. In addition, a rubric could include questions about the learning process such as, "What problems did you confront while making your project?" or "What were your significant learnings while making the project?" Examples of forms and assessment tools for projects and presentations follow. See Table 4.2 for a rubric example that teachers may use to evaluate student projects.

PROJECT PROPOSAL FORM
(Minnesota New Country School project form, revised by Mary Jost)

For group or individual project

NAME(S) and Homeroom advisors:
1._____
2._____
3._____
4._____

Title of Project:_____

Identify the topic to be investigated:

List at least 3 questions you would like to answer concerning your project:

1._____

2._____

3._____

How would this project make your community/world a better place?

What help from other teachers/subjects might you need?

Tasks/Activities necessary to complete this job and person in group who will be responsible. Give a brief explanation on the task, if necessary. It should be clear to your advisor what you are trying to accomplish.

List a minimum of three different resources you will use. At least one of these must be a primary source (living person).

1._____

2._____

3._____

Tentative time line

Project Advisor*—You will need to periodically check in with your advisor over the course of the project. List at least three tentative dates that you will meet with your advisor to discuss your progress. (Advisor will initial upon completion of each check-in.)

1.   advisor's initials ____
2.   advisor's initials ____
3.   advisor's initials ____

Parent/Guardian Signature #1 I/We have discussed this project with my/our student.

_____

Parent/Guardian Signature #2 I/We believe our student's project is ready for final approval.

_____

*Project Advisor = Teacher assigned to guide the student in the project and does not necessarily refer to the Homeroom advisor.

Project Proposal Form (River Bend Academy)

Name: Date:

Others (if group project): _____ _____ _____

Title of the Project: _____

Planning the Project

I. Identify the Problem or Issue. Answer the question, "What do you already know?"

II. List at least three (3) basic information questions you would like to answer about your project.
    1.

    2.

    3.

    4.

III. How does your project affect your life outside of school? What makes this project important to the community or world around you?
    1.

    2.

Project Content

IV. Develop a web or an outline to define and organize your project. (Attach it to this proposal.)

V. List the Tasks/Activities/Steps needed to complete this project:
    Complete by date:
            (If the project is a group project, identify the activities
            each person is responsible for completing.)

_____
_____
_____
_____
_____
_____
_____
_____
_____
_____

VI. List at least three (3) different types of resources that you will use for your project, other than the Internet. Make sure to talk to a person as one of your resources.
1.

2.

3.

VII. List the high standard areas that you expect to work in to complete this project. (Attach a copy of these areas after you have highlighted them.)
1.
2.
3.
4.

VIII. What will be your final product(s)? (Examples: report, poster, Power-Point presentation, model, article, etc.)
1.
2.
3.
4.

IX. Proposed Project Credits (Must document hours and learning to receive credit): _____

X. Initial Proposal Approval:

Parent/Guardian _____ Date _____

Advisor _____ Date _____

Project Planning Team

_____ Date _____

_____ Date _____

_____ Date _____

<u>After</u> Project is Completed

XI. Final Project Checklist (Complete these items before meeting with the Project Assessment Team)
    _____ 1. Timelog (total your hours before the meeting)
    _____ 2. Documentation of Learning
    _____ 3. Web/Outline
    _____ 4. Report/Writing Piece
    _____ 5. Final Product/Visual (poster, display, PowerPoint presentation, photos, etc.)
    _____ 6. Project Assessment Form
    _____ 7. Project Rubric
    _____ 8. Money Spent (Budget)
    _____ 9. Bibliography

XII. Final Project Approval

I agree that this project is ready for final approval.

Peer Signature_____ Date _____

Parent/Guardian _____ Date _____

Advisor _____ Date _____

Project Assessment Team

_____ Date _____

_____ Date _____

_____ Date _____

# of Documented Hours _____   Letter Grade Earned _____

Project Credits Granted _____   Rubric Score _____
Insert forms here

Artifact Form
Learning Log:
  List number of minutes you worked on the project in class.

  Write down the minutes you worked on the project outside of class.

  Parent Signature _____

References:
  List articles, book titles, and authors used.

  List titles of videos used.

  Provide notes from conversations and/or interviews conducted.

Websites:
  List website addresses used.

List materials needed to build the project.
  1.
  2.
  3.
Keep drawings of your plans and/or the project.

Project Assessment and Personal Reflection Form
River Bend Academy Charter School
Mankato, Minnesota, 2001

Name _____ Date _____

Title of the Project _____

Objectives

Conceptual Goals: What are some of the most interesting and important facts you learned about your topic?

Process Goals: What specific skills did you learn, practice, or master while working on your project?

Affective Goals: How has working on this topic affected you as a student, citizen, and/or a member of your family?

Personal Reflection

What went well during your project? Explain why it went well.

What did not go well during the completion of your project? Explain your answer.

Table 4.2. Disciplined Inquiry for Project-Based Learning

Rubric Descriptors*	Novice	Acceptable	Admirable	Exemplary
	The performance or project is ineffective. The performance is unpolished, providing little evidence of planning, practice, or consideration of audience. The presentation is unclear and confusing so that key points are difficult to determine.	The performance or project is somewhat effective. Some problems with clarity, thoroughness, and delivery are evident. It is unclear whether the audience, context, and purpose have been considered.	The performance or project is effective. Ideas are presented in a clear and thorough manner, showing awareness of the audience, context, and purpose.	The performance or project is highly effective. Ideas are presented in an engaging, polished, clear, and thorough manner. A high-quality craftsmanship is evident and is mindful of the audience, context, and purpose.
	1	2	3	4
Disciplined Inquiry for Project-Based Learning: Project Demonstration				
Disciplined Inquiry for Project-Based Learning: Reflective Written Expression				

MAXIMIZING THE LEARNING

Relevancy or usefulness of the project is important when implementing this teaching approach. If one of your goals is to encourage ongoing problem solving using a project as the vehicle, then the project should be relevant and useful to the student. The miniature catapult and wooden boat that were used in previous examples are projects that require some problem solving, but how relevant are they to students? Students will undergo a problem-solving process by creating a plan, testing it, and reflecting on how well it worked, but once this is complete, learning may come to a halt.

Class competitions to determine how far a ball can be thrown by a catapult or how far a small wooden boat travels across a pool of water tend to be short-lived projects, and once the competition is over these projects no longer serve a purpose and will probably be discarded. In such situations, learning how to build a better catapult and boat ceases.

Although these projects do engage students in problem solving, there are other projects that may engage students in a continuous process of problem solving that lasts beyond the class and possibly for years into the future. For instance, someone interested in fishing could do a project that leads to a long-term process of problem solving in designing and building effective fishing lures. At first the lures might be rather crude and ineffective, but as one continues to redesign them, they would become stronger and more effective in catching certain fish. Building a lure may not be a one-shot project in which it is built, tested, and discarded. The procedure of making lures could become an ongoing problem-solving process of planning, testing, reflecting, and redesigning to make them better.

To help maximize learning, educators might encourage students to create projects that are interesting and useful to them. Making a backpack, building a straightening iron, or designing a web page may be more relevant projects than a catapult or small wooden boat. When you tap into students' interests, the learning may continue long after the class or semester is over.

RESOURCES

Website Resources

The Mummified Chicken, Mutant Frogs, and Rockets to the Moon: An Introduction to Project Based Learning from the Student Perspective. EdVisions Inc. 507–248–3738, http://www.edvisions.com.
WestEd: http://www.wested.org/pblnet/exemplary_projects.html.
EdVisions Schools: http:/www.edvisions.com.

Print Resources

Markham, T., Larmer, J., & Ravitz, J. (2003). *Project based learning handbook: A guide to standards-focused project based learning for middle and high school teachers.* Novato, CA: Buck Institute for Education.

Newell, R. (2003). *Passion for learning: How project based learning meets the needs of 21st-century students.* Lanham, MD: Scarecrow Press.

Railsback, J. (2002). *Project based instruction: Creating excitement for learning.* Portland, OR: Northwest Regional Educational Laboratory.

Chapter Five

Service-Learning

Service-learning is a well-known experiential approach to the teaching/ learning process that has been utilized for decades by multitudes of schools, youth agencies, and education-related organizations. It is probably the most familiar approach among those presented in this book, and therefore, perhaps the least likely, when mentioned in public conversation, to be followed with the comment, "Service-learning? What is that?"

In spite of its familiarity, misconceptions still exist that use the term *service-learning* to refer to service of any kind for any reason. Although volunteer work and service projects are intent on fulfilling community needs, the main beneficiary is the recipient of the service. Only when service *and* learning are mutually emphasized does service-learning occur. Generally, service-learning entails three requisite phases: (1) planning to fill a community need, (2) action, and (3) reflection (Berger Kaye, 2004). By emphasizing all three components, it is easy to see that service alone (the action) without the intentional educational aspects (planning and reflection) would not meet the accepted criteria for service-learning. By slightly shifting one's thinking of the term from service-learning to *learning from service,* it further becomes evident that the focus is the learning that comes from the service experience, and not simply the service. The learning that results is either equally or more important than the service itself.

A fourth phase that is often added is presentation or demonstration, meaning an intentionally planned way for the learners involved in the experience to share with others what they accomplished and learned. This also provides an opportunity to share ideas for future service opportunities they would like to experience. Some educators refer to the four stages as *preparation, action, reflection,* and *demonstration,* and use the acronym, *PARD,* to describe the formula or model they use to implement service-learning (Berger Kaye, 2004). A slight twist to this last phase is to add some way of evaluating the quality of the experience or the level of performance of the learners. In this case, the acronym, *PARE,* has been used, with the "E" representing evaluation rather than demonstration (Gupta, 2006).

In spite of situations where all of the PARE/PARD elements are implemented, the emphasis placed on each may vary. The service-learning typology developed by Sigmon (as presented in Furco, 1996) is especially helpful in revealing different foci that could result in drastically different experiences for the learners (Table 5.1).

A universal definition of service-learning does not exist; a selection of several definitions are offered here to indicate both the commonalities that run through them and the insightful variances in perspective of the person or agency that created them:

- "A teaching method where guided or classroom learning is deepened through service to others in a process that provides structured time for reflection on the service experience and demonstration of the skills and knowledge acquired" (Berger Kaye, 2004, p. 7).
- "Service-learning unites academic study and volunteer community service in mutually reinforcing ways. The service makes the study immediate, applicable, and relevant; the study, through knowledge, analysis, and reflection, informs the service" (International Partnership for Service-Learning and Leadership [ISA-NSLC], 2008, n.p.).
- "Service-learning relates academic study to work in the community in ways that enhance both" (University of Colorado at Boulder Service Learning Office, 2008, n.p.).
- "Service-learning is a teaching and learning strategy that integrates meaningful community service with instruction and reflection to enrich the learning experience, teach civic responsibility, and strengthen communities" (Learn and Serve America's National Service-Learning Clearinghouse, 2008, n.p.).

Table 5.1.   Service-Learning Typology

Service-LEARNING	Learning goals are primary; service outcomes are secondary.
SERVICE-learning	Service outcomes are primary; learning goals are secondary.
Service learning	Service and learning goals are completely separate.
SERVICE-LEARNING	Service and learning goals are of equal weight and each enhances the other for all participants.

Source: Sigmon (as presented in Furco, 1996).

• "Service-learning is an educational experience based upon a collaborative partnership between college and community. Learning through service enables students to apply academic knowledge and critical thinking skills to meet genuine community needs. Through reflection and assessment, students gain deeper knowledge of course content and the importance of civic engagement" (Berea College Service-Learning Advisory Committee, 2004, n.p.).

The use of service-learning over the past few decades has grown by leaps and bounds to the point where the federally funded Corporation for National and Community Service (CNCS) (2008) claims to have generated 3.9 million volunteers in 2007 through its three main service programs: AmeriCorps, Learn and Serve America, and Senior Corps. CNCS was allotted a respectable $885 million operating budget in fiscal year 2007. The President's Higher Education Community Service Honor Roll is also sponsored by CNCS. In 2007, 528 colleges were recognized on the Honor Roll list for "extraordinary contributions to service in their communities" (Learn and Serve America, 2008a, ¶ 1).

From preschool through college, schools across the United States have incorporated service-learning into their curricula and, at increasing numbers, into their mission statements or identified core principles. Volunteering among college students alone increased over twenty percent between 2002 and 2005 (Corporation for National and Community Service, 2006). The current literature on service-learning is broad and comprehensive. Due to its versatility across all disciplines, its associated research base is also speedily gaining strength. Although its increased usage over the past few years may lead some to think of it as a fairly new educational method, service-learning has a long history in this country. The following section examines that history more closely.

HISTORY

The term *service-learning* was coined by Robert Sigmon and William Ramsey during the early 1960s. They were educators and intentionally created the term to emphasize educational experiences where both learning and meeting human needs took place (Titlebaum, Williamson, Daprano, Baer, & Brahler, 2004). The year 1966 is also identified as the year that the term was first used when it was applied to describe a Tennessee Valley Authority project involving college students in the eastern Tennessee area (LSA-NSLC, 2008).

It is well recognized, however, that the history of service-learning begins well before the term was ever coined. Events that took place in the late 1800s such as the Morrill Act of 1862, which allowed for land grant colleges; the Chautauqua Movement, which offered adult home study groups for over five decades; and Chicago's Hull House, established in 1889 to provide free housing and education for the needy are all examples that are included in early service-learning endeavors (Titlebaum et al., 2004). In 1910, William James, noted American philosopher, advocated in *The Moral Equivalent of War* for a national service venue that would involve America's youth in ways separate from the military (LSA-NSLC, 2008). A few years later, national cooperative extension services were made possible by the passing of the Smith Lever Act in 1914 to enable colleges to develop and provide knowledge and instruction in agricultural, rural energy, and home economics for their local communities (Titlebaum et al., 2004).

Although the Civilian Conservation Corps (CCC) established by President Franklin Roosevelt may not have fulfilled the educational emphasis of service-learning, it was probably the largest service endeavor ever undertaken inside the boundaries of the United States. From 1933 through 1942, the CCC brought millions of unemployed young men together with the land "in an effort to save them both" (Titlebaum et al., 2004, n.p.) through erosion control and conservation efforts in the country's natural areas.

In 1961, the same year that he became president, John Kennedy established the Peace Corps for the purpose of extending peace and friendship from U.S. citizens to people who live in the poorest areas of developing countries around the world. A part of the legislation wording for the Peace Corps emphasized reciprocity of understanding between the people and cultures involved (LSA-NSLC, 2008). Not long after, in 1964, President Lyndon Johnson signed the Economic Opportunity Act that established Volunteers in Service to America (VISTA), a program originally envisioned by John Kennedy (AmeriCorps, 2008). VISTA sent thousands of volunteers to provide service in poor neighborhoods in California, Connecticut, and Appalachia, to name a few. VISTA spread its services to all states and eventually merged with the Peace Corps. It is now a branch of AmeriCorps, operating under the Corporation for National and Community Service.

In 1967, Robert Sigmon and William Ramsey, coiners of the term *service-learning*, established the Manpower Development Internship Program, which was specifically designed to promote both educational growth for the service provider, and fulfill a community need for the service recipient (Titlebaum et al., 2004). This was followed in 1969 by the Atlanta Service-Learning Conference, which was sponsored by VISTA; the Peace Corps; U.S. Department of Health, Education, and Welfare; and other southern regional educational entities. This gathering was described as hosting "one of the first formal attempts" (n.p.) to define service-learning. At the conference, the Southern Regional Education Board crafted the definition of service-learning as "the integration of the accomplishment of tasks that meet human needs with conscious educational growth" (n.p.).

Continuing to gather public interest and support, service-learning experienced another boost at the national level with the implementation of the Youth Conservation Corps in 1970 by the U.S. Department of Agriculture. During its first year, it reportedly hired thirty-eight thousand youth. This program hires young people, ages fifteen through eighteen, to work and learn together while fulfilling service projects on public land (National Park Service, 2008).

Throughout the remaining years of the 1970s and the 1980s, several additional service-learning–focused agencies were organized, including the Young Adult Conservation Corps, the National Center for Service-Learning for Early Adolescents, the National Youth Leadership Council, the Campus Outreach Opportunity League, and Youth Service America (Titlebaum et al., 2004). One of the agencies that emerged in 1985 was National Campus Compact, initiated by the presidents of Brown, Stanford, and Georgetown Universities. The mission of Campus Compact (2008) is to unite college presidents to promote citizenship through public and community service among their students. Campus Compact remains a vital player in service-learning nationally; it claims to work with 1,144 campuses and has branches established in thirty-three states as of 2007.

The CNCS (2008) was created in 1994 as a part of the National Service Bill. Three programs, AmeriCorps, Learn and Serve America, and Senior Corps, operate under CNCS. AmeriCorps is popular among college students and draws participants each year to provide service in the areas of public safety, health, the environment, and education. The main focus of Learn and Serve America (2008b) is to provide support for service-learning to K–12 schools, colleges, and various community groups. Senior Corps (2008) organizes people over fifty-five years of age for providing service such as mentoring, companionship, foster grandparenting, and job skills to those in need. Also, in 1994, Congress passed a bill that declared the celebration of Martin Luther King Day as a day of service and charged the CNCS with organizing service endeavors on that day.

In 2001, the Learn and Serve America National Service-Learning Clearinghouse was established as an additional function of CNCS for the purpose of collecting and disseminating information on all facets of service-learning

(Titlebaum et al., 2004). Finally, in 2001, the first international conference was held in Berkeley, California, funded through a grant from the W. K. Kellogg Foundation and chaired by Andrew Furco. The conference still continues today, and now is a function of the International Association for Research on Service-Learning and Community Engagement (2008), an entity that was newly established in 2005.

These early initiatives on the part of people and agencies motivated to promote service and learning helped to create an educational method that is applauded and participated in by multitudes across the country and around the world today. Because of the immense growth of service-learning throughout all disciplines in schools and colleges, the research body pertaining to service-learning is increasingly showing positive results. The next section provides an overview of some of the recent research that concentrates on learning outcomes.

WHAT THE RESEARCH SAYS

Most educators who utilize service-learning agree that it "helps young people have a greater likelihood of achieving a sense of self" (Berger Kaye, 2004, p. 215), strengthens citizenship (Constitutional Rights Foundation, 2008), and increases academic performance (Astin, Vogelgesang, Ikeda, & Yee, 2000). Those who support service-learning and believe it enhances the educational experience often do so intuitively, without the need to read piles of research studies that show this to be true. Billig acknowledges, "Research in the field of service-learning has not caught up with the passion that educators feel for it" (2000, p. 660). However, because educational methods are continually scrutinized and educators are held accountable for student achievement, it helps to be able to assure administrators, parents, and colleagues that service-learning does, in fact, increase student learning.

A seminal study conducted by Conrad and Hedin in 1991 (as discussed by Billig, 2000) conducted a meta-analysis on the research that existed at the time on service-learning. They concluded that there was quantitative evidence, albeit limited, that service-learning made a positive impact on learning. The qualitative evidence derived from student and educator perspectives was stronger. In the years since the Conrad and Hedin study, characteristics of American youth have changed from being less likely to volunteer than other age groups to now being more likely than other age groups (Billig, 2000). There was a disconnect back then of youth to government, voting, politics, and society at large.

Today, young people are voting in increasingly larger numbers, are interested in national and global events, and are more engaged in community grassroots initiatives. In reference to the decade following Conrad and Hedin's study, Billig claims service-learning has "grown by leaps and bounds" (2000, p. 659), as evidenced by findings that twenty-seven percent of U.S. high schools in 1984 offered service programs compared with eighty-three percent in 1999. Surely that percentage has continued to increase.

One of the most extensive studies conducted this decade on service-learning entailed quantitative data collected from 22,236 undergraduate students at nineteen U.S. colleges over a four-year period. In-depth, qualitative data was collected from a subsample drawn from three of the participating campuses. Astin et al. found significant correlations between service-learning participation as a part of a college course and academic performance, values solidification, self-efficacy, leadership, choice of careers in service fields, and plans to engage in service activities after leaving college (2000, p. ii). Astin et al. further identified a multitude of other studies that confirmed similar findings (p. 1, 2). In this same study, interest in the topic of the service project was the "single most important factor associated with a positive service-learning experience" (p. iii). This is important to note! Equally significant is that the second most important influencer was class discussion encouraged by the instructor after the service event was completed. If instructors often bridged the class content with the service-learning experience, understanding of the course material also increased. The qualitative data from the study revealed that students and educators alike increased their sense of civic responsibility and self-efficacy through service-learning experiences (p. iv).

Furco and Billig (2002) reported on several studies presented at the first International Service-Learning Research Conference held in 2001 that substantiated the findings of Astin et al. (2000). In addition, they summarized recent research that emphasized the importance of flexibility in service-learning projects, meaning that there should be opportunities for learners to provide feedback during the project and also make adjustments if problems arise that could prevent the experience from being a positive one.

These various research studies also indicate that a "developmental fit" (Furco & Billig, 2002, p. 95) should be carefully constructed, matching the service-learning requirements with the physical and emotional capabilities of the learners. A further finding discussed by Furco and Billig found that short-term service-learning projects did not appear to result in long-term beneficial effects. This places a challenge on the shoulders of educators to implement longer projects or to implement projects more often, and to implement projects that align with the previous suggestions.

In addition to the research discussed in the previous paragraphs, multitudes of research studies have been conducted that identified service-learning as especially appropriate for academically gifted students (Lee, Olszewski-Kubilius, Donahue, & Weimholt, 2007), for at-risk youth (Nelson & Eckstein, 2008), for first-year college students (Stavrianopoulos, 2008), and for children during their early childhood years (Swick, 2001). Equally large numbers of studies reveal increased academic achievement when used in teaching specific disciplines. The point here is that there is ample research available today to support the claim that service-learning is for all learners and all subject areas.

HOW TO USE SERVICE-LEARNING

At the beginning of this chapter, four phases were introduced as necessary components for effective and successful service-learning events. The acronyms PARE or PARD represent these parts: preparation/planning, action, reflection, and evaluation or demonstration. For simplicity, PARE will be used in this section to show various ways of using these four phases.

Preparation and Planning

The first step in preparation is deciding on the service project or projects that will take place. The decision-making process depends on how much time is available for this stage, on the extent that the service-learning will play in the curriculum, and on the age group. Ideas for projects may come from a list of possibilities that have already been compiled by a local government, university, or community agency, or perhaps have been generated from previous knowledge of a community need. There are also many online sources available for generating ideas. A fairly new online resource is a tool from Learn and Serve America's National Clearinghouse website. The tool is called Service-Learning Ideas and Curricular Examples (SLICE), and is a searchable database of projects, lessons, and syllabi. If time allows, the projects may be determined after investigation by the students of the various needs that are prevalent in their community.

Preparation also involves becoming informed about the service topic. Common topics include the environment, homelessness, hunger, literacy, immigrants, seniors and the elderly, safety awareness, animals, and medical concerns. Gathering knowledge about the topic can involve reading, field trips, guest speakers, films, newspapers, and interviews. Students should know going into a service-learning experience some of the underlying causes that created the community need, some of the past and current endeavors to resolve the need, and the demographics and characteristics of the people who are most affected by the need. They should also be familiar with the agency that they will be working with during the service project—its mission, its history, and from where it derives its funding.

Depending on the service project chosen, an action plan may need to be developed by the students. There may be schedules that need to be arranged and different tasks that need to be divided among small groups. Finally, preparation includes all of the logistics that need to be in place for the event such as transportation, materials, chaperones, particular clothing, food, drink, and a back-up plan in case weather is a concern.

Action

The action phase will obviously be more successful if the preparation leading up to it has been thorough. In anticipation of the reflection step that follows, learners can be encouraged to make observations of their own behavior during their experience and to be cognizant of what they think they are learning along the way.

Depending on the age group of the learners and the extent of the service project, the instructor may or may not be present during the actual service activities. If the instructor is present, it may be best to roam around, checking on different groups, and being available to solve problems or observe individual and group performance. Other times, it may be right for the instructor to take part in the activities, to model for and help motivate students.

Reflection

One of the key components of service-learning is reflection—the stage where learning outcomes are identified and the experience advances from just service to service-learning. This is also where transfer of learning begins to take place from the current experience to future learning situations. During reflection, learners recall what they accomplished, identify feelings and emotions, and attach meaning to and conceptualize what they experienced. There are various ways to guide the students through reflection, and, with experience, instructors will learn what works best for certain types of experiences and certain ages of learners.

Whatever type of reflection activities are implemented, it is important to ensure that reflection is facilitated in a way that retains emotional safety for all learners. If reflecting verbally in a group format, establishing ground rules first is recommended. Some commonly used rules are (1) everyone gets a turn, (2) everyone is listened to respectfully without interruptions or put downs, (3) everyone has a right to pass (meaning that no one should be forced or coerced into speaking out loud).

Specific reflection sessions often involve answering open-ended questions crafted by the instructor to provide a place to discuss what happened and draw out the important aspects of the service experience. These questions may be answered in oral or written form, and individually or in partners or in small groups. Shorter reflection sessions (five to ten minutes) are more successful with younger ages or groups with shorter attention spans. With older secondary or college students, reflection sessions may remain at enthusiastic levels for an hour or more. The purpose of the questions and subsequent discussions is to mindfully guide the learners in self-identifying the relevance and growth that occurred. Some potential questions to get started are provided here, but the possibilities of reflective questions are endless.

- What was my general schedule of activities today? What did I do first, second, and so on?
- What activities were the highlights for me? What made them positive?
- What activities were not among my favorites today? What made them so?
- Did I feel comfortable or uncomfortable during my experience today?
- How well did I perform my job or tasks today?
- How well did I cooperate with others?
- What kind of impression did I make on the people I was serving or helping?
- How satisfied am I with my experience today?
- What could I have done to make today more positive?
- What do I think are the main things I learned today about myself? About others? About the people who live in my community?
- Am I interested in more service-learning projects in the future?
- If I were to participate in another service-learning project, would I want to do something similar or provide a different kind of service next time?
- If I were to participate in another project, what would I want to remember from today to help me have a positive learning experience next time?

In addition to reflective questioning sessions, there are other venues for helping students to reflect on their service projects. Journaling is among the most common of individual reflection activities. Journaling may involve responding to specific questions such as those posed previously, or may simply be an outlet for free writing of whatever comes to mind regarding the service experience. Journals are especially helpful and appropriate when learners will be participating in several service-learning opportunities over time. They are also a convenient way to involve everyone when time for reflection may be limited during class time or when the entire group is not easily gathered at the end of a service event. Journals can also be taken home and turned in another day. It should be noted that a comprehensive study of over twenty-two thousand undergraduate college students found that journaling by itself did not increase learning to the same extent as reflection that included peer dialogue about the experience (Astin et al., 2000).

Props of various kinds are sometimes helpful catalysts for reflection, too, and can easily be made from inexpensive materials. One example is to cut out several pictures and images from old magazines and ask learners to choose one that represents something from their experience that day. This may be slipped into their journal and remain private, or they may share with their peers what they chose and explain the reasons why they chose that particular image.

Another prop example is to blow up a beach ball and write an emotion on each section of the ball or all over the ball such as "nervous," "uncertain," "confident," "satisfied," "happy," or "sad" on it. Toss the ball around and ask students to choose the emotion that most closely resembles what they felt before the service project started, how they feel now that it is completed, and the reasons why.

A third example is to point to various parts of the body to represent different aspects of the experience. For example, point to your eye and ask, "What was something you saw today that made an impression on you?" Point to your ear and ask, "What was something you heard today that you've never heard before?" The heart represents something that was touching or evoked a strong emotion. The brain represents something that was thought, but not said. Hands represent someone who deserves applause or someone who lent a hand. Feet represent something that moved the job or task forward or someone who led the way. The mouth represents something that was profoundly spoken or something that brought a smile to others.

The main thing to remember with reflection is to plan it with particular objectives in mind, and then to make sure enough time is provided for it. A rushed or deleted reflection session can be what makes the difference between a successful service-learning experience and one that leaves learners lost and disappointed.

Evaluation

The evaluation phase includes evaluation by both the students and the instructors, and even sometimes by the recipients of the service. The depth and breadth of evaluation depends on how integrated service-learning is into the particular class or curriculum through which it took place—whether it is a one-time event or an ongoing series of events throughout a semester or year.

The purpose for the evaluation is also important to consider, and determines what the instructor needs to assess. Will the service-learning be used as a graded assignment? Will the service event be followed by another at the same place, and therefore require evaluation to improve aspects of it for next time? Will the event be followed by a more involved project covering a longer length of time, and therefore require more careful preparation?

One aspect of evaluation that is often encouraged is an opportunity for the students to demonstrate or present to others what they feel were the most important aspects of their learning experience. This may take place in front of other class members, or perhaps parent groups, community groups, or other school-related groups. To add the dimension of applying their learning to new situations, students are often asked to also identify future service-learning opportunities they would like to experience and why.

Davis, Miller, and Corbett (1998) produced a comprehensive manual, available online through Florida's Learn and Serve America website, devoted to evaluating service-learning activities. The manual provides several qualitatively and quantitatively oriented options and sample forms for evaluation. The qualitatively oriented pieces include instructor observations of individuals and groups, rubrics, students' assessments of what they experienced, and ways to assess student journals and portfolios. A few of the blank forms, slightly adapted, that seem to be the most widely applicable are offered in Figures 5.1, 5.2, 5.3, and 5.4. They can easily be altered for use with various age groups. The manual also provides forms that have been completed as examples for instructors.

MAXIMIZING THE LEARNING

An admirable school-wide initiative for at-risk adolescents described by Nelson and Eckstein (2008) helps reveal *what's possible* in service-learning. Teachers at an alternative secondary school in the southwestern United States involved their students in the grant-writing process for community service grant funding through the U.S. Department of Education and the No Child Left Behind Act. Small groups of students identified community needs and projects, then determined costs, time lines, and logistics to carry out the projects. Their grant proposals were formally

Name: Date:

Service Site:

Activity you participated in:
Think about your experiences while working at your service-learning site today. Please be
honest in your responses. You input is valued and will be used to improve future service-
learning projects at this site. Please check the appropriate boxes below.

Yes	No Opinion	No	
			The activities were well organized.
			The job/task requirements & directions were clear.
			There were enough jobs/tasks for everyone.
			Adequate supervision was provided.
			All materials needed were available.
			The job/task I performed served a worthwhile purpose.
			I enjoyed working on my assigned job/task.
			I would have like to have been able to try different jobs/tasks.
			I had the opportunity to learn something new today.
			I had the opportunity to teach someone something new today.
			I enjoyed working with my group today.
			I had some trouble getting along with others in my group today.
			I feel that I did something positive for my community today.
			I was able to help plan the activities for today.
			I think students should plan the activities for each day.

Figure 5.1.   Student Evaluation of Service-Learning Activity
Source: Adapted from Davis, Miller, & Corbett, 1998.

Service Site: Date:

Activity your group participated in:

Group members: 1.

                 2.

                 3.

                 4.

                 5.

Things we liked about this project:	Things we would change:

Figure 5.2.   Group Evaluation of Service-Learning Activity
Source: Adapted from Davis, Miller, & Corbett, 1998.

Name:

Date and Time:

Observer:

Site/Service Project:

Observations of events and behaviors:

Comments/Summary:

Figure 5.3.   Instructor and Student Anecdotal Observation Record
Source: Adapted from Davis, Miller, & Corbett, 1998.

Date and Time:

Observer:

Site/Service Project:

Behavior	Name	Name	Name	Name
Cooperation				
Communication with others				
Motivation				
Ability to work independently				
Use of time				
Willingness to follow directions				

Figure 5.4.   Group Anecdotal Observation Record
Source: Adapted from Davis, Miller, & Corbett, 1998.

presented to a "service-learning advisory board" (p. 230) made up of students, teachers, and administrators who determined which grants would be funded. In this particular grant cycle, a playground for a local Salvation Army and the renovation of a neighborhood park were funded and the projects completed with all students in the school involved.

In an ideal service-learning world, learners will be key players in the entire service-learning experience such as the case study reported by Nelson and Eckstein (2008) reveals. It is an admirable challenge for educators to provide the time and relinquish control to allow for experiences that are totally student-driven. However, such an ideal situation may be quite difficult to achieve in most educational settings that are limited by short class periods, field trip restrictions, transportation costs, liability concerns, and chaperone requirements.

Undoubtedly, higher interest and motivation will exist in the service experience if the students are involved in the decision-making process as to what the service-learning will entail. This can become problematic, however, if it is necessary for an entire class or group of students to take part in the same experience and the group is split on what they want to do. Taking a majority vote or compromising can result in some students harboring ill feelings toward the experience, the agency, the people being served, or each other. What will be an educative event for some will be a mis-educative event for others.

Therefore, although this may run counter to the tenets of experiential education, sometimes it is beneficial for educators to arrange a *first* service-learning experience for their particular group with little student input in terms of what the service will be and where it will take place. This may be especially appropriate for younger groups. This way, a service project can be arranged that will provide all the learners in a class or group with the same shared experience, and educators may guide it in a way that will result in a positive learning experience for all.

Going through a first experience together helps learners to build relationships and strengthens group dynamics during the planning and action stages of the project. It also allows for the reflection and presentation stages of service-learning to be demonstrated and discussed all together, showing students how to reflect, how to bring what they learned to their consciousness, and apply that learning to future situations. By using this guided-discovery approach with students through their first service-learning experiences, they can attain the skills, in part or full, that they need to effectively plan future experiences on their own.

An additional idea to maximize learning is to constantly encourage students to plan further service-learning experiences either as individuals or in small groups. If it is more comfortable for them, they could return to the same place they went for their first experience, and fulfill a similar or different type of service that is needed there. A list of possible places that welcome service-learning students could be provided for students to choose from. Many universities have service-learning or community service offices that have such lists available. Or, if students are ready, they can be encouraged to research what community needs exist and try something totally new. The educator can further maximize learning by providing incentives for completing additional service-learning projects, such as special recognition or extra credit points for each hour of service provided on one's own initiative.

There are many resources available to help educators maximize their students' learning as much as possible. Several are listed in the following section that provide research findings, teaching guides, lesson plans, and project ideas.

RESOURCES

Website Resources

The International Partnership for Service-Learning and Leadership: http://www.ipsl.org

Learn and Serve America: http://www.learnandserve.gov/Default.asp

Learn and Serve America's National Service-Learning Clearinghouse: http://www.servicelearning.org

National Service-Learning Partnership: http://www.service-learningpartnership.org

Service-Learning Network, a free e-newsletter published by the Constitutional Rights Foundation: http://www.crf-usa.org/

Synergy, a free e-newsletter published by Washington Campus Compact: http://www.wacampuscompact.org/

Print Resources

The Generator: A Journal for Service-Learning and Youth Leadership, published by the National Youth Leadership Council.

Information for Action: A Journal for Research on Service-Learning for Children and Youth, published by the National Service-Learning Partnership.

Journal for Higher Education, Outreach, and Engagement, published by the University of Georgia.

Michigan Journal for Community Service-Learning, published by the University of Michigan.

Chapter Six

Place-Based Learning

So bountiful hath been the earth and so securely have we drawn from it our substance, that we have taken it all for granted as if it were only a gift, and with little care or conscious thought of the consequences of our use of it; nor have we very much considered the essential relation that we bear to it as living parts in the vast creation. (Liberty Hyde Bailey, 1915/1980, p. 5)

When we see land as a community to which we belong, we may begin to use it with love and respect. (Aldo Leopold, 1949/1987, p. viii)

Place-based education is, at its core, exactly what it sounds like—learning focused on particular places. There are additional dimensions, however, that propel its definition beyond an approach that improves learning to an approach that improves life. Promise of Place has defined it as "a holistic approach to education, conservation and community development that uses the local community as an integrating context for learning at all ages" (2008a, ¶ 1). Several sources agree that place-based education is intent on enhancing the vitality of the community, while simultaneously supporting the health of the environment and strengthening student achievement.

A SHIFT FROM FAR TO NEAR

A main tenet of place-based learning is that it is "rooted in what is local—the unique history, environment, culture, economy, literature, and art of a particular place" (Rural School and Community Trust, 2003, ¶ 1). This has not always been the case. With its strong environmental education roots, place-based education often concentrated on rural or ecological contexts (Cole, 2007; Graham, 2007). Over time, the purpose of place-based education has shifted from the development of a concern for the natural environment *out there somewhere* to the development of partnerships between schools and their communities with an underlying value for local environmental health. It is "inherently tailored by local people to local realities" (Promise of Place, 2008a, ¶ 1). Although it is implemented close to home, an intended outcome is to serve as a springboard for understanding the major issues of the global community, and the local community's role in responding to those issues (Center for Place-Based Education, 2008, ¶ 2).

One catalyst for the shift of focus from environments far from home to those that are local was the recognition that urban environments can and do ignite people–place relationships that are as strong as, if not stronger than, those ignited by rural environments. Motivation for learning was found to be higher when it involved places where learners already had a degree of "interest, curiosity, or knowledge" (Sarkar & Frazier, 2008, p. 30). The importance of one's own place or the learner's place supplanted the importance of a natural or wilderness place to which the learner had no previous, and possibly no future, connection. This shift was accompanied, albeit slowly, by the belief that future concern for far-away, natural places would develop as a sense of one's place eventually rippled into other place relationships.

It is now accepted that place-based learning can occur anywhere, whether it be in urban, suburban, or rural contexts (Sarkar & Frazier, 2008, p. 30). What is important is that it is localized in the learner's environment. The premise is that when learners develop connections to their own place and have adequate levels of skills and opportunities to act, they become more actively participative in their communities. The more community involvement there is, the more the local social capital increases, resulting in healthier communities (Powers, 2004).

TENETS OF PLACE-BASED EDUCATION

Promise of Place (2008b) and the Place-Based Education Evaluation Collaborative (PEEC) (2003) are two agencies that work closely together and present very similar wordage on the main principles of place-based education. The following bulleted list is a combined and partial paraphrase from their respective websites.

Place-based education:

- Is personally relevant to learners.
- Is interdisciplinary.
- Takes place on the school campus, local community, and nearby environments.

- Focuses on local themes, systems, and content.
- Contributes to the community's vitality and environmental quality.
- Works in partnership with local organizations, businesses, and government.
- Is tailored to local audiences.
- Is grounded in the development of a strong and personal concern for one's place.

These tenets are broad enough to encompass all subjects and grade levels. Simultaneously, they are narrow enough to provide educators with a focus for what place-based learning is and is not.

THE NEED FOR PEOPLE–PLACE RELATIONSHIPS

Place-based education has experienced recent renewed attention largely due to the growing outcry against the federal No Child Left Behind (NCLB) Act of 2001 (U.S. Department of Education, 2008) and the timely publication of Richard Louv's (2005) book, *Last Child in the Woods*. NCLB and its four pillars of accountability—state freedom, community freedom, proven practices, and parental choice—were intended to narrow the achievement gap for school children from specified lower achieving groups. Although supporters of NCLB claim it has been successful, critics of the Act (including several state governments) and its associated high-stakes testing have argued that it has actually lowered achievement standards and resulted in teaching to the test at the expense of desirable curricular emphases other than reading, writing, and mathematics (Ebersole & Worster, 2007; Gruenewald, 2003).

David Sobel, who has a strong voice in the place-based education literature, has gone so far as to suggest NCLB is sending us on a "pathway to educational purgatory" (2008, p. 8). Similarly, Louv asserts, "When we challenge schools to incorporate place-based learning in the natural world, we will help students realize that school isn't supposed to be a polite form of incarceration, but a portal to the wider world" (2007, ¶ 10).

In reaction to the NCLB Act of 2001 and its tendency to cause teachers to teach only what will be tested (therefore sacrificing outdoor environmental education), a new federal bill has been introduced and has been gaining admirable attention. The No Child Left Inside (NCLI) Act was first introduced and passed in the Senate in 2007 as S.B. 1981 and was approved by the House of Representatives in September 2008 as H.R. 3036. Supporters of the bill claim the problems of childhood obesity, detachment from nature, climate change, and a narrowing curriculum due to NCLB have led to a need for this act (No Child Left Inside Coalition, 2009).

NCLI amends and extends two previous laws that influence environmental education in schools: the Elementary and Secondary Education Act of 1965 and the National Environmental Education Act of 1990. If passed, NCLI will provide grant funding for various agencies to provide teacher professional development in environmental education and for states to develop environmental literacy standards and curricula. As of this writing, over one thousand state and national agencies across America have joined the coalition in support of NCLI (No Child Left Inside Coalition, 2009).

Detachment from nature has been identified as a major concern for the future of the earth and its children. Louv makes a strong case for getting our nation's children back into the outdoors, away from their sheltered indoor lives and technology-oriented pastimes, ultimately rescuing them from what he calls a "de-natured childhood" (2005, p. 31) or "nature-deficit disorder" (p. 34). His main concern, as is true for place-based learning, is for the betterment of the child (or learner). However, he asks a crucial question, "Where will future stewards of nature come from?" (p. 145), which underscores the environmental sustainability values embedded in place-based learning endeavors.

Louv (2005) also advocates for creating *green cities* either from the ground up or by building intentional green spaces within existing urban and suburban areas. The future leaders of our cities will not desire to do so, however, unless an affinity for nature is developed in our children now. Place-based education is one part of the solution for igniting the desire and subsequent action plans to creative living spaces that bring us closer to natural places.

HISTORY

Going far back in time, seventeenth-century educational reformer John Amos Comenius was a proponent of learning about places by experiencing them rather than reading about them. He also was a believer in learning about things closer to home before learning about things farther away (Knapp, 2005). There have been countless others, however, before and after Comenius's time who promoted the importance of living close to the land, making it a complex task to pinpoint the beginning of place-based learning. The Rural School and Community Trust has aptly described it as "simultaneously a new and an old idea" (2003, ¶ 7). The history presented here focuses on people and events from more recent times, mainly from the 1900s, that shaped this approach to learning.

Use of the Term

Place-based education, called as such, emerged as an outgrowth of environmental education in the 1960s and 1970s. PEEC (2003) identified four instrumental initiatives that contributed to the evolution of place-based education: the Foxfire Fund, begun in the 1960s; Education for Sustainability, begun in the 1980s; the Annenberg Rural Challenge, begun in the 1990s; and Stories in the Land Teaching Fellowships, offered since the early 1980s through the Orion Society.

David Sobel is a faculty member at Antioch University New England and the director of the Center for Place-Based Education there. He is often credited as one of the originators, if not the main originator, of what is now known as *place-based education.* He himself claimed that it was the Orion Society that first used the term *place-based* to describe this particular approach in the early 1990s (Sobel, 2005). Place-based education (also called *place-based learning, community-based learning,* and, to a lesser extent, *place-conscious learning* or *pedagogy of place*) is closely associated with and has roots in the idea of building a *sense of place,* a term that has also surfaced in the past few decades. The following paragraphs present some of the contributors who developed a sense of place and people–place education, as well as offer a brief discussion on an emerging outgrowth known as a *critical pedagogy of place.*

Sense of Place

One premise of place-based learning is that one's social identity and ecological identity are born out of one's environment, or significant surrounding places (Ebersole & Worster, 2007). With American families increasing their residential mobility and amount of time spent inside, locked away from the outside world, the result is a degree of "placelessness," or lack of a sense of one's place in or ability to contribute to the larger world. This, in turn, forms social and ecological identities that are stunted, apathetic, or unrecognizable at a conscious level.

Many environmental writers over the past several decades have written about their own development of a sense of place, although they may not have used that terminology. They have likewise encouraged the importance of land ties for others, often especially in connection to children and schooling. Among these authors are Ernest Thompson Seton, Henry David Thoreau, Annie Dillard, Liberty Hyde Bailey, Anna B. Comstock, John Muir, Aldo Leopold, and Sigurd Olson. Their contributions to the importance of a sense of place are too vast to cover in this chapter. However, it would be remiss not to highlight the influence of Aldo Leopold, who wrote prolifically about the necessity to reconnect people with the land.

Leopold (1949/1987) was an American forester, professor of wildlife management, and politically active environmentalist throughout the first half of the twentieth century. He is renowned for his writings on the importance of developing a collective "land ethic" (p. 221), which he described as "the existence of an ecological conscience [which] in turn reflects a conviction of individual responsibility for the health of the land" (p. 221). Healthy land is that which has the capacity for self-renewal. Human practices, he contended, prevent that capacity far too often. He lamented the destructive land practices that he had observed throughout his years working in forestry, farming, hunting, wilderness use, and soil management.

In 1935, Leopold founded the Wilderness Society (2008), an agency devoted to promoting a land ethic and protecting wild places. Leopold (1949/1987) asserted that developing a land ethic involves both an intellectual process of learning and knowing what impacts the earth, but also an emotional process of connection to the land and a desire to care for it. Similar to the views of John Dewey, discussed in the following section, Leopold surmised, "Perhaps the most serious obstacle impeding the evolution of a land ethic is the fact that our educational and economic system is headed away from, rather than toward an intense consciousness of land" (p. 223).

Dewey, Pestalozzi, and Rousseau

Much of what has been written in the last few decades about place-based education references educational philosopher John Dewey (1900/1990) who, over a century ago, bemoaned the isolation that resulted from schools teaching content that was separate from all that children knew and lived and held as meaningful. In the Lab School at the University of Chicago, Dewey and his associates attempted to forge connections between schools and communities and the children who belonged to both. He believed education should be based on lived experiences; likewise, life provides a most excellent context for educative experiences (Dewey, 1900/1990; Smith, 2002).

In alignment with Dewey's views, place-based learning "aims to work against the isolation of schooling's discourses and practices from the living world outside the increasingly placeless institution of schooling" (Gruenewald, 2003, p. 620). One of many scholars of place-based learning who blames schools themselves for distancing children from the places in which they live, Gruenewald suggests that schooling has been cut "off from the pulse of cultural life and experience" (2003, p. 625). He further states:

Because the structures and processes of schooling are based on institutional patterns of isolating teachers and students from places outside school, one can claim that schools limit experience and perception; in other words, by regulating our geographical experience, schools potentially stunt human development as they help construct our lack of awareness of, our lack of connection to, and our lack of appreciation for places.

Although Dewey is attributed as the originator of many of the educational methods he espoused, he often expressed that they were not his unique ideas. Dewey (1916/1997) self-admittedly was influenced by Johann Pestalozzi, a renowned Swiss educator in the 1700s, who regularly took his school children on ventures away from the school grounds for the purpose of learning and living in the outdoors. In turn, Pestalozzi was inspired by Jean Jacques Rousseau, and more specifically, his book, *Emile,* a novel about a private tutor who teaches a young boy, Emile, by experiencing the outdoors and using leading questions to help the boy derive answers and knowledge from within himself (Gutek, 1968, 1991).

Both Pestalozzi and Rousseau believed that society was corrupt and was oppressively entrenched in classism. Taking children outdoors to learn helped to equalize and free them from those societal constrictions (Gutek, 1968, 1991). Dewey concurred with Pestalozzi and Rousseau's stances against oppressive practices in education. Although this does not appear in the place-based literature, it is suggested here that an unspoken core value of place-based learning is that it is for everyone because everyone can (and should) have places they care for that are special, sacred, and provide relief from daily worries, problems, and inequities.

Critical Pedagogy of Place

A newer wave of place-based learning is cresting as recognition has increased that social and ecological identities are greatly intertwined with the places and spaces with which we interact on a daily basis, rather than places far removed. That recognition was logically connected to a movement away from limiting place-based education to solely wilderness or rural contexts, since most people live in urban or suburban environments. Several place-based scholars now support the idea of a critical place-based pedagogy that combines ecological, place-based education with the social justice values of critical theory (Cole, 2007; Graham, 2007; Gruenewald, 2003; Ruitenberg, 2005). Critical pedagogy of place seeks to detect and bring to light ways that inequality, cultural differences, power imbalances, and political agendas can lead to environmental depletion and destruction (Gruenewald, 2003).

WHAT THE RESEARCH SAYS

The Children and Environments Center for Research and Design in Denver claims many beneficial outcomes of place-based education that include higher test scores, grades, critical thinking abilities, motivation, and more responsible environmental behavior (Chawla & Escalante, 2007). Because most place-based endeavors occur with classroom-sized groups, and often involve several episodes over longitudinal periods, much of the existent research is not generalizable across the board to all place-based programs. However, the body of research is leading to a growing indication of positive educational results study by study, program by program over time.

Research from Overlapping Approaches

Ann Powers (2004) is a cofounder of Program Evaluation and Education Research Associates (PEER). She works closely with PEEC to evaluate place-based programs, and admits that research specific to place-based learning had "been slim" up to that point (p. 18). However, she explains, decades of research in related areas helps to substantiate the effectiveness of place-based learning. For example, the work of developmental theorist Jean Piaget reveals that engagement increases and children learn better when they are intrinsically motivated and active. Andrew Powers and PEER Associates (2008) assert that growing research in closely related (often overlapping) educational approaches, such as service-learning, also provide evidence of the effectiveness of place-based learning. They state that "the great volume of research in service learning is certain to offer great practical value to practitioners of [place-based education]" (p. i).

Place-Focused Research

Through her work with PEER, Ann Powers conducted a cross-program research study in 2004 on four specific place-based programs that are in partnership with PEEC. The study involved two whole-school change programs and two professional development programs for teachers. There were 163 educators interviewed. Various other forms of data were collected as well. Powers established the importance of teacher buy-in and adequate training as paramount to implementing successful programs. All four programs that were studied revealed these beneficial changes in teachers: (1) increased use of local places and resources, (2) interdisciplinary teaching, (3) teacher collaboration, (4) leadership and personal growth, (5) stronger curriculum planning skills, and (6) increased use of service-learning (2004, p. 24). What was found, in other words, was that teachers began to exhibit many behaviors that have been associated with effective teaching overall (i.e., leadership, collaboration, interdisciplinary planning).

Although impact on teachers (rather than students) was the main focus of the study, Powers (2004) also discovered that students with special needs consistently performed at higher levels when involved in place-based activities. They worked more independently, were more enthusiastic, and gained increased respect from their regular-education peers. For all students associated with the study, learners claimed to work harder and were more attentive to their studies when they understood they were helping their community. Some students reported learning more when there was a relevant purpose to their schooling. There was also evidence that some students demonstrated higher levels of responsibility and maturity.

An intriguing study conducted with public schools in Boston compared fourth grade standardized test scores of children who attended schools with renovated outdoor recreational areas, gardens, and school yards with those who attended schools with dilapidated or unusable outdoor spaces (Lopez, Campbell, & Jennings, 2008). Scores revealed significantly higher achievement in math for students at the schools with the renovated spaces, and slightly higher achievement in language arts. Lopez et al. concluded that the higher scores were a result of either improvement in the physical environments or increased physical activity by the students as a result of the environmental improvements, or both. Although further research is warranted, since the students were actively involved in the renovation of the outdoor spaces at their schools, this study suggests that people–place relationships were strengthened and resulted in higher student achievement.

Environment as an Integrating Context

There is an extensive body of research that has been conducted on schools or programs that use the environment as an integrating context for learning, often referred to as *environment as an integrating concept (EIC)*. These programs may or may not focus on the development of people–place relationships; however, many of the associated studies provide admirable evidence of increased student achievement that can be correlated with place-based education. A study of four hundred high school students in Florida found significant increases in achievement motivation in ninth and twelfth grade learners who were involved in an EIC curriculum compared with those who were not (Athman & Monroe, 2004).

In 2000, the National Environmental Education and Training Foundation (NEETF) published the results of its extensive study on several EIC programs and schools across the United States. NEETF claimed higher reading and math scores on standardized tests and higher achievement in science and social studies. Students were better able to transfer learning "from familiar to unfamiliar contexts" (2000, p. 4). Motivation to learn science increased. Discipline problems declined. Finally, teachers consistently reported that students who usually performed at low levels were able to perform at increasingly higher levels with EIC lessons. NEETF concluded overall that learners were more engaged and enthusiastic, and displayed more pride and ownership in their accomplishments when involved in EIC-focused curricula.

HOW TO USE PLACE-BASED LEARNING

One of the main pieces of advice given by various educators who use place-based learning is to begin with an interdisciplinary mindedness, moving outside of the science and ecologically focused traditions of early place-based educational endeavors. A good starting point is to find out what place-based initiatives are taking place across the country at various grade levels and across various disciplines. The Antioch New England Institute (2008), a branch of Antioch University New England, promotes environmental sustainability and civic engagement. The Institute's home page provides links to several current programs, several of which are involved in place-based learning. Most of the links to these programs provide detailed examples of the projects in which their students and clients are involved.

Getting Started

The Place-Based Landscape Analysis and Community Education (PLACE) program (2008) recommends that educators try to plan across three realms of place. These are the physical landscape (topography, geology, climate, water ways), the cultural landscape (the people, and their history and culture), and the ecological landscape (all of the organisms that live there and how they interact in their environment).

If educators feel they have limited knowledge in some of these areas, they can enlist community experts (or amateur enthusiasts) to share their knowledge and lead students in various activities. One example of starting simply and using local expertise is to pose a single intriguing question such as, "Where do wild edible berries grow in this community?" A community member with knowledge about berries may agree to take students on several excursions to collect berries, or students might research on their own where to locate, identify, and collect the berries. This can lead to further learning experiences such as jelly making, preserving of foods through canning and drying, and medical treatments for plant poisoning or improper preservation of foods. Further place-based investigations may emerge such as identifying other wild edibles and poisonous plants, map making to document where these plants grow, and studying soils and climate that allow wild edibles to grow where they do.

For more ideas, the following five-tiered approaches recommended by Smith (2002) provide dozens of possibilities for investigations of place:

- Cultural studies (native versus current inhabitants, immigration, history, tradition and ceremony, art, landscapes, religion, gender, ethnicity, class, recreation, communication, grassroots organizations, housing).
- Nature studies (local natural flora and fauna, invasive species, introduced species, soil, water, air, land, environmental threats and issues).
- Real world problem-solving (identifying and investigating actual school and community issues—political, cultural, social, economical, health and safety).
- Internships and entrepreneurial opportunities (identifying what possibilities exist in the local community for students after school, during summer break, or upon high school graduation to get involved in local events, organizations, and businesses; creating more of these by seeking out partnerships).
- Induction into community processes (local economics, urban renewal projects, service projects, community decision making).

In reference to induction into community processes (the last bullet), Smith (2002) offers several actual examples of students helping with local decision-making processes. He described a city that was interested in upgrading its local playgrounds. A group of elementary school children helped in the process by surveying other children on their preferences for playground equipment. Another example involved a fire department that wanted to know if its local citizens changed their smoke detector batteries each year at the beginning of daylight savings time. A group of middle school students surveyed citizens to find the answer. Yet another group of secondary students surveyed their peers on their discretionary spending and discovered most of it was spent outside the immediate community. This helped local merchants to alter the products they offer, enticing more spending closer to home.

Finding Places by Walking Around

Once an educator understands the breadth of possibilities, the next step is to locate where various learning experiences can or should take place. Sarkar and Frazier suggest that the first step is to go out and walk around the school grounds and neighborhood looking for "the possibilities [they] offer in terms of researchable questions" (2008, p. 31). Teachers can then formulate investigative questions on their own or plan potential questions with their students, depending on their objectives, timeframe, or their comfort level with place-based learning.

Based on their own experience, Sarkar and Frazier encourage teachers to present questions to their students in the fall semester, and then have students generate their own questions in the spring from the data they previously examined.

Border Investigations

Similar to walking around to generate ideas, Giesbrecht (2008) used a border walking exercise to introduce her college students to place-based strategies. She wanted to help them develop a relationship with their campus and neighborhood that went beyond thinking of them as areas that were simply walked through to get to classes. She asked them to walk alone within a few blocks' radius of the perimeter of the campus and bring back one artifact found along their journey. Once the students returned, they shared their experiences and their artifacts, generating questions as to what meanings the artifacts held, what they represented about the community surrounding the campus, and what their walk did to add to a deeper (or beginning) knowledge of the neighborhood in which they went to school. These insights, in turn, led to generating questions about what they would like to investigate to learn more about the surrounding neighborhood and environment. This exercise could easily be adapted for use with younger learners walking as a group with their teacher, and especially holds the potential for people–place relevance if the children live in the neighborhood surrounding the school.

One Hundred Miles from Home

An additional idea to help educators get started with place-based learning is the "100 mile curriculum" (Giesbrecht, 2008, p. 27). It is a growing practice for people to limit their diets, in full or part, to food grown locally, often meaning food that is grown within 100 miles of their home. Giesbrecht extended this idea through a challenge to her colleagues to concentrate their curricula, no matter what subjects they taught, on issues, resources, and communities that existed within a 100-mile radius of the school. Examples of the creative ideas her colleagues came up with included examination of (1) gentrification through a cultural and historical lens, (2) a local river-bottom forested ecosystem, and (3) recreational impact on local lakes. For elementary students, the 100-mile radius could be greatly reduced, or a number of blocks used or street borders designated rather than mileage. Spending a school year (or semester) investigating as many natural and human-created phenomena as possible within 100 miles (or other boundaries) would surely result in enormously deep and broad knowledge about one's place.

MAXIMIZING THE LEARNING

David Sobel (2008) has identified seven design principles that should serve as focal points for strengthening children's relationships with nature. These principles are derived from Sobel's observations of ways that all children naturally play when they have the free time to do so. It is within these "play motifs" (p. 21), he asserts, that "transcendent experiences occur" (p. 21), where children's emotions and feelings expand into behaviors and actions.

Why wouldn't educators, Sobel (2008) reasons, design lessons and curricula that provide venues for these innate ways that children play, learn, and experience the world? Motivation for this type of play-like learning is already built in. There is no need for educators to struggle to engage their students. Learning is naturally maximized, as these are the ways of learning that have already been chosen by children. Sobel's seven principles (Table 6.1) offer a brief explanation of the premise of each one. Although Sobel's intention was for these activities to make people–nature connections, many of them can also be utilized in less natural places to build people–urban place connections as well.

Some additional ideas for maximizing learning have been recommended by Molly Baker, codirector of the Outdoor Education program at Colgate University, who advocates for a return to Aldo Leopold's *landfullness* rather than *landlessness* (2005, p. 267). She proposes four themes that form the "landfull framework" (p. 272) to help move land from being viewed as merely a backdrop—from something people travel through or over to something people travel with and in (p. 271). The four themes, which can be used in order as levels or can be inter-mixed, are (1) being deeply aware, (2) interpreting land history, (3) sensing place in the present, and (4) connecting to home. Guiding learners through answering questions related to each of the four themes develops well-rounded perspectives and multiple ways of understanding one's interdependence with the land.

Being Deeply Aware

Use sensory awareness, mapping, observation, and beauty appreciation types of activities to address these questions:

1. Where am I?
2. What is around me?
3. Who is around me?

Table 6.1. Design Principles for Place-Based Learning

Adventure	Children love action combined with challenge; they need opportunities to stalk, balance, jump, and scamper in order to develop strong mind–body connections.
Fantasy and Imagination	Children love to live out their dreams and imaginations; they need opportunities for stories, plays, puppet shows, and dramatic play to enable them to experience (albeit imaginatively) the challenges, successes, and complexities of life "rather than just study them" (p. 24).
Animal Allies	Children have a natural attraction to animals; they need opportunities to touch them, build kinship with them, and understand their unique behaviors before they can learn scientific facts about them and develop an ethic of caring for them.
Maps and Paths	Children love to follow clues on treasure maps, explore new paths, and discover what is around the next corner; they need opportunities to create and use their own maps in order to understand geographical regions and connect their usefulness to finding real places.
Special Places	Children seek out and create special places such as forts, tree houses, and clubhouses; they need unstructured time, space, and resources to create their own special retreats where they can imagine living out historical traditions of resourcefulness, ecological impact, bartering, tribes, and territories.
Small Worlds	Children love to create miniature neighborhoods and spaces that "they can play inside of" (p. 45) such as doll houses, sand boxes, and train sets; they need opportunities to create tiny worlds in order to understand bigger, abstract ecosystems.
Hunting and Gathering	Children love to gather and collect almost anything, especially hidden treasures; they need opportunities for connecting clues and hunting treasures (sometimes treasures of knowledge) in order to develop skills in researching and mining resources.

Interpreting Land History: Natural and Cultural History

Use site-specific interpretation, journaling, role playing, skits, drama, and imaginary time travel types of activities to address these questions:

1. How has this land changed over time?
2. What and who lived here in the past?
3. How did they relate to the land?

Sensing Place in the Present

Use map-making, terrain naming, solo experiences, and creative art types of activities to address these questions:

1. How is this place unique?
2. Who lives in or passes through this land now? What is their relationship to it?
3. What does this place mean to me?

Connecting to Home

Use activities such as water source investigation, documentation of daily navigation from home to school or work, envisioning the town or neighborhood long ago, and comparing discoveries found on a trip to similar things back home to address these questions:

1. How can this place link to other landscapes and experiences with land?
2. When does the land become home?
3. When does home become the land?

The Rural School and Community Trust sponsored a document, *Assessing Student Work,* which provides a plethora of alternative assessment ideas, meaning assessment strategies other than testing and writing papers. One idea that fits well with place-based learning is a pre- and postactivity survey to help learners and educators assess the changes in awareness, knowledge, and affective realms that are occurring as place-based lessons are experienced. The survey in Figure 6.1 offers a shortened version adapted from the document (Harvard Documentation & Assessment Program, 2001).

Whatever activities are used, to maximize learning there should be a mindful intentionality for helping learners to build relationships with places from multiple perspectives. Knowing only the physical properties, or the history, or who lives there now can result in half-formed, short-term relationships or relationships that are founded on a false sense of entitlement and inappropriate decisions for future use of the land. Keeping in mind that building relevant people–place relationships; increasing student learning; and helping to build sustainable, healthy communities are all objectives of place-based education, educators can plan for lessons and activities that will make tremendous differences in the lives of their students and the future leaders of their communities.

Strongly Disagree				Strongly Agree		(√ = pre-experience, O = post-experience)
1	2	3	4	5	6	
	√			O		I have a strong and personal attachment to a particular community.
√		O				I often discuss or think about how political, social, or national issues affect the community.
	√			O		I participate in political or social causes that help improve the community.
			√	O		I benefit emotionally when I do things that contribute to the community.
		√		O		It is my responsibility to help improve the community even if it is hard work.
		√		O		I am aware of some of the important needs of the community.
				√O		Providing service to the community is something I like to do.
				√O		I have a lot of personal connection with people in the community.
	√	O				I feel I have the power to make a difference in the community.
		√		O		I try to encourage others to participate in community service.
		√		O		I believe I can personally make a positive difference in the community.
√		O				I believe I have enough influence to impact community decisions.

Figure 6.1. Pre- and Post-Community Awareness Survey
Source: Harvard Documentation and Assessment Program, 2001.

RESOURCES

Website Resources

Center for Place-Based Education, Antioch New England Institute, Keene, New Hampshire: http://www.antiochne.edu/anei/cpbe.

A Forest for Every Classroom: http://www.nps.gov/mabi/forteachers/forest-for-every-classroom.htm

Place-Based Education Evaluation Collaborative: http://www.peecworks.org/index

Promise of Place: http://www.promiseofplace.org

Sustainable Schools Project, Shelburne Farms, Shelburne, Vermont: http://www.sustainableschoolsproject.org/index.html
The Rural School and Community Trust: http://portfolio.ruraledu.org/
Vermont Education for Sustainability: http://www.vtefs.org

Print Resources

Orion Society. (1998). *Stories in the land: A place-based environmental education anthology.* Great Barrington, MA: Orion Society.
Rural School and Community Trust. (2003). *Place-based learning portfolio workbook.* Henderson, NC: Rural School and Community Trust.
Sobel, D. (2005). *Place-based education: Connecting classrooms and communities.* Great Barrington, MA: The Orion Society.
Sobel, D. (2008). *Childhood and nature: Design principles for educators.* Portland, ME: Stenhouse Publishers.
Walker Leslie, C., Tallmadge, J., & Wessels, T. (1999). *Into the field: A guide to locally focused teaching.* Great Barrington, MA: Orion Society.

Chapter Seven

Thoughts on Assessment

Have you ever asked yourself what the purpose of assessment is? Why do we assess student learning? Is it to determine who the top five, the middle fifteen, and the bottom five are in the class? Is it to prove to parents that their sons and daughters are learning things from day to day, semester to semester, and year to year? Is it to prove that your students and classes are making adequate progress in your school? Or is it for the primary purpose of acquiring state funding and holding teachers accountable?

The primary purpose of assessment should be to help students understand what they have learned, and that learning is limitless and should be a lifelong endeavor. Unfortunately, educators sometimes get mired down with all the policies and procedures associated with assessment and lose focus on what really matters most: student learning.

The process of grading can be especially derailing to student learning. Educators can easily get caught up in the details of how to grade students and become more concerned with the process of grading than the goal of learning. Grade inflation, for example, causes some educators to feel uneasy about doling out too many As, resulting in a situation where they look for ways to "mark down" students.

We have been in conversations with educators who seem to weigh certain questions unfairly in order to bring down test scores. One question that requires a one-word answer may be worth ten points, whereas another one-word answer on the same test is worth one point. There seems to be a lack of standardization from one teacher to the next on how they determine point values for test questions. Using tests to assess student learning might appear to provide an objective measurement, but the way in which questions are weighted can be arbitrary and subjective, depending on the teacher. Some educators intentionally find ways to lower grades so they will not be accused of handing out too many As.

Many schools now have websites where parents can view their children's assignments, scores, and grades. These websites look like grade books (in some cases, they probably are grade books), with lists of points awarded for tests, quizzes, turning in assignments on time, and so on. These types of assessment tools focus primarily on what students have already learned, and are based on summative assessment techniques.

Summative assessment relies mostly on tests and grades to describe what students have "learned" from answering questions correctly. It does not provide opportunities to improve upon what was learned or provide information on how students can learn better. Unfortunately, summative assessment relies on external motivators such as points and grades, which usually do not have a lasting impact on students.

Stiggins, Arter, Chappuis, and Chappuis argue that "in our current system assessments and grades are used to engineer compliance, deliver evaluative feedback (grades, which many students receive as a judgment of themselves and their worth as people), and compare students to each other (engendering negative competition and thus reinforcing a judgment of self-worth)" (2006, p. 39). Students may remember the information long enough to provide correct answers on tests, but usually they forget it rather quickly because it has no relevancy or meaning to their lives. They practice reciting information in their heads to remember answers for test questions because they are afraid of consequences such as failing grades, parental and teacher disappointment, and limiting their possibilities for college admittance and college scholarships. There appears to be tremendous pressure placed on students to motivate themselves to remember large amounts of information that they don't care about or has little meaning to them.

If external motivators such as grades were deemphasized and learning focused on demonstrating knowledge in ways other than taking tests, then educators could allow more time for students to practice what they are learning, resulting in better-educated students who could solve problems and think for themselves. If the goal of education truly is student learning, then a shift needs to occur in how educators view learning. We need to move away from having students memorize information to having them learn how to solve relevant problems, which will better prepare them for life.

Formative assessment is different than summative assessment in that it is a process used to improve student learning and teacher effectiveness, and often relies on demonstrating what has been learned in ways other than testing. It moves the teacher and student into the future and looks at what changes need to be made in order to improve learning. Popham defines formative assessment as "a planned process in which teachers or students use assessment-based evidence to adjust what they are currently doing" (2008, p. 6). Formative assessment is dynamic and helps students understand what they have learned, as well as what they still need to learn and how to improve upon their learning.

Formative assessment is aligned with experiential learning and focuses on learning specific types of skills. "What types of skills?" you might ask. According to Pearlman (2009), today's students need to learn life skills such as critical thinking, problem solving, and communication that will prepare them for life and allow them to compete in the future. He poses a question that asks if students who have passed their state's exit exam mandated by the No Child Left Behind Act will be successful as citizens and workers in the twenty-first century, and his answer is "not a chance" (¶ 1). He argues that today's world requires students to acquire more complicated skills that need to be practiced and refined over time. Rather than assessing students on content standards associated with all the different subject areas, educators should be assessing life skills that will equip students to tackle difficult challenges they will face in their lives.

In many cases, this defines experiential learning. Students practice a skill until they learn how to do it with some proficiency, or create and refine a product until they get it correct. This may require trial-and-error episodes, but with each attempt students are practicing their problem-solving skills.

With experiential learning, students demonstrate their knowledge and are evaluated on their performance, not their ability to memorize information. While memorizing information could be classified as a skill, it is not a particularly useful one because students can quickly access information that is readily available through the Internet and other sources. The need to memorize content information is diminishing at increasing rates as the capabilities of the World Wide Web continue to grow.

Being able to find information and understand how to apply it, on the other hand, are useful skills that learners need. Students should be given multiple opportunities to practice and improve upon these types of skills while still in school so they will be adequately prepared for life now and after graduation.

Wurdinger and Rudolph's (2009) research on a project-based learning school in Minnesota showed that students and alumni were learning more about life skills than academic skills through their projects and presentations. The alumni surveyed in this study felt that acquiring these life skills gave them advantages over their college classmates (92 percent), and coworkers (83 percent), and allowed them to reach their goals after graduation (92 percent). What types of skills were they learning? By doing projects and presenting them to their advisory committees, students learned skills such as creativity, problem solving, decision making, time management, finding information, and learning how to learn, which are highly valued in today's work environments. This research provides evidence that schools should intentionally attempt to teach students these types of skills to prepare them for life.

With experiential learning, remembering information long enough to score well on a test is not the goal; one has to apply the information, integrate it, and make sense of how it relates to one's life. Learning life skills is a byproduct of experiential learning. When students are involved in any of these five approaches, they learn about life skills because they are challenged to think critically, solve problems, and create meaningful projects and products that are relevant and useful. It may be more challenging to assess experiential learning because students are involved in using a variety of life skills, but there are tools that may be used to assess all five of the methods mentioned in this book. Prior to identifying these tools, it is necessary to discuss what we are attempting to assess when students are involved in these five approaches.

Stiggins et al. (2006) discuss several types of learning targets; two that are specific to experiential learning are skills and products. They give examples of skills, which include reading, public speaking, playing an instrument, using laboratory equipment, and conducting investigations (p. 64). We classify these as technical skills that are easy to observe and assess. However, there are other sets of skills such as problem solving, creativity, critical thinking, being a team player, and communication, which we classify as life skills, that are equally important to learn and should be incorporated into curriculums. Products are things like construction projects, papers, websites, and portfolios.

Popham (2008) also discusses learning targets and believes that there is only one target that should be assessed. He suggests that educators should assess "a skill (rather than a body of knowledge) and usually a significant skill at that—the kind of learning outcome requiring a number of lessons for students to achieve it" (p. 24). Popham (2008) and Stiggins et al. (2006) both argue that learning requires doing something with knowledge and that skills and products require direct experience with the subject matter. One cannot learn a skill simply by reading a book; the information in the book must be applied. Skills and products are the primary learning targets that should be assessed with these five approaches.

Stiggins et al. (2006) and Popham (2008) also argue that formative assessment should occur over time. Mastering skills and creating products take time, and in order for students to improve upon their learning they need to know where they are currently, where they are going, and how they can get there. For instance, with communication skills, students could watch a video of their first presentation and compare it to an exemplary presentation in order to understand what they need to work on to reach a higher level of proficiency. With each successive presentation, students could be working on developing better content, clarity, flow, and eye contact to improve their communication skills. The formative assessment process allows educators and students to make adjustments along the way that will help enhance learning over time.

A summative assessment could be used to identify where students are with their skill levels, but should not stop with one score on that particular skill. Instead, this same skill should be practiced throughout the course and assessed at different times to show how the students have improved over time. Too often educators assess knowledge or skill of a particular subject and then move on to the next without discussion of what students can do to improve their knowledge or skill of the original subject. Formative assessment allows students to adjust their learning, make corrections, and increase their skill throughout the entire course.

All five approaches in this book focus on the acquisition of skills, products, or a combination of the two. Active learning and problem-based learning, for example, could focus primarily on strategies that promote classroom discussion, so communication, organization, and problem solving are three skills that educators could assess with these two methods. Project-based learning, service-learning, and place-based education, on the other hand, often include a combination of products and skills. For example, skills such as teamwork, communication, and creativity can be assessed when small groups create a website, and, in addition, the website could also be assessed.

Students engaged in these five approaches may also need to learn research skills such as searching library databases so they can find necessary information that helps them solve the problems they have been assigned. These five approaches are rich in learning, and each individual educator will need to identify specific skills and products that they want to assess prior to beginning the learning process.

Rubrics are probably the best tools for assessing skills and products. There are an abundant number of rubrics on the Internet and educators can adapt them to assess both the technical and life skills mentioned previously. There are also numerous rubrics that assess products and projects. Rubric websites where one can find numerous rubrics on skills and products are listed under the Resources section in this chapter. These sites have hundreds of rubrics that can be adapted for your own classes. They also have rubric templates that allow educators to personalize their own unique assessments. With a little creativity and practice, educators can design rubrics to assess skills and products for their classes.

Unlike paper-and-pencil tests, the key to formative assessment is to identify the skills to be learned and allow multiple opportunities for students to
practice them over time. The first time students solve a problem in a group,
present a project, or create a product such as a website in your class might
result in a low score on a rubric, but with practice students should be able to
improve their skills over time. A low rubric score on problem-solving abilities should transform into a higher score by the end of the course. Educators
who focus on teaching students technical and life skills, and use rubrics to
assess them, will find that students can learn technical and life skills, which
will equip them to not only become effective, successful members of society,
but lifelong learners as well.

RESOURCES

http://www.ncsu.edu/midlink/ho.html
http://www.rubistar.com
http://www.shambles.net/pages/staff/rubrics/
http://www.tcet.unt.edu/START/instruct/general/rubrics.htm
http://www.teach-nology.com/

References

AmeriCorps. (2008). *The history of AmeriCorps VISTA.* Retrieved July 14, 2008, from http://www.americorps.org/about/programs/vista_legacy.asp.

Antioch New England Institute. (2008). *Understanding Antioch New England Institute.* Retrieved August 19, 2008, from http://www.anei.org/index.cfm.

Astin, A.W. (1993). *What matters in college? Four critical years revisited.* San Francisco: Jossey-Bass.

Astin, A., and Oseguera, L. (2002). *Degree attainment at American colleges and universities.* Los Angeles: University of California, Higher Education Research Institute.

Astin, W. A., Vogelgesang, L. J., Ikeda, E. K., and Yee, J. A. (2000). *How service learning affects students.* Los Angeles: University of California, Higher Education Research Institute.

Athman, J., and Monroe, M. (2004). The effects of environment-based education on students' achievement motivation. *Journal of Interpretation Research, 9*(1), 9–25.

Bailey, L. H. (1915/1980). *The holy earth.* Ithaca: New York State College of Agriculture and Life Sciences, Cornell University.

Baker, M. (2005). Landfullness in adventure-based programming: Promoting reconnection to the land. *Journal of Experiential Education, 27*(3), 267–276.

Barak, M., & Dori, Y. J. (2005). Enhancing undergraduate students' chemistry understanding through project-based learning in an IT environment. *Science Education, 89*(1), 117–139.

Barkley, E., Cross, K. P., and Howell Major, C. (2004). *Collaborative learning techniques: A handbook for college faculty.* San Francisco: Jossey-Bass.

Barron, B., Schwartz, D., Vye, N., Moore, A., Petrosino, L., Zech, L., and Bransford, J. (1998). Doing with understanding: Lessons from research on problem and project-based learning. *The Journal of the Learning Sciences, 7*(3), 271–311.

Beebe and Masterson. (2006). *Communicating in small groups.* Boston: Allyn & Bacon.

Berea College Service-Learning Advisory Committee. (2004). *What is service-learning?* Retrieved July 10, 2008, from http://www.berea.edu/celts/servicelearning/.

Berger Kaye, C. (2004). *The complete guide to service-learning.* Minneapolis, MN: Free Spirit Publishing.

Billig, S. H. (2000). Research on K-12 school-based service-learning: The evidence builds. *Phi Delta Kappan, 81*(9), 658–664.

Blackburn, R.T., Pellino, G. R., Boberg, A. and O'Connell, C. (1980). Are instruction improvement programs off target? *Current Issues in Higher Education, 2*(1), 32–48.

Blumenfeld, P., Soloway, E., Marx, R., Krajcik, J., Guzdial, M., and Palincsar, A. (1991). Motivating project-based learning: Sustaining the doing, supporting the learning. *Educational Psychologist, 26*(3&4), 369–398.

Bonwell, C., & Eison, J. (1991). Active learning: Creating excitement in the classroom. ASHE-ERIC Higher Education Report No. 1. Washington, DC: The George Washington University, School of Education and Human Development.

Bonwell, C., and Sutherland, T. (1996). The active learning continuum: Choosing activities to engage students in the classroom. In T. Sutherland and C. Bonwell (Eds.). *Using active learning in college classes: A range of options for faculty* (pp. 3–16). San Francisco: Jossey-Bass.

Bransford, J. D., Brown, A. L., & Cocking, R. R. (Eds.) (1999). *How people learn: Brain, mind, experience, and school.* Washington, DC: National Academy Press.

Bridgeland, J., Dilulio, J., and Morison, K. (2006). The silent epidemic: Perspectives of high school dropouts. Washington DC: Civic Enterprises LLC.

Brookfield, S. D. (2006). *The skillful teacher.* San Francisco: Jossey-Bass.

Brookfield, S., and Preskill, S. (2005). *Discussion as a way of teaching.* San Francisco: Jossey-Bass.

Bruce, B. C., and Davidson, J. (1996). An inquiry model for literacy across the curriculum. *Journal of Curriculum Studies, 28*, 281–300.

Campus Compact. (2003). *Introduction to service-learning toolkit: Readings and resources for faculty.* Providence, RI: Brown University.

Campus Compact. (2008). *2007 service statistics: Highlights and trends of Campus Compact's annual membership survey.* Providence, RI: Campus Compact.

Cannon, M. D., Griffith, B. A., & Guthrie, J. W. (2006). Effective groups: Concepts and skills to meet leadership challenges. New York: Allyn & Bacon.

Cauley, K. M., and Jovanovich, D. (2006). Developing an effective transition for students entering middle school or high school. *Clearing House, 80*(1) 15–25.

Center for Place-Based Education. (2008). Retrieved August 2, 2008, from http://www.antiochne.edu/anei/cpbe.

Chawla, L., and Escalante, M. (2007). *Student gains from place-based education.* Denver, CO: Children, Youth, and Environments Center for Research and Design, University of Colorado at Denver. Retrieved August 20, 2008, from http://www.cudenver.edu/Academics/Colleges/ArchitecturePlanning/discover/centers/CYE/Publications/Documents/Factsheet2.pdf.

Chickering A.W. (1977). *Experience and learning: An introduction to experiential learning.* New Rochelle, NY: Change Magazine Press.

Cohen, E. (1986). *Designing group work.* New York: Teachers College Press.

Cole, A. G. (2007). Expanding the field: Revisiting environmental education principles through multidisciplinary frameworks. *Journal of Environmental Education, 38*(2), 35–44.

Concept to Classroom. (2008). *Inquiry-based learning workshop.* Thirteen Ed Online. Retrieved on July 22, 2008, from http://www.thirteen.org/edonline/concept2class /inquiry/index.html.

Constitutional Rights Foundation. (2008). *What is service learning?* Retrieved August 25, 2009, from http://www.crf-usa.org/service-learning.

Cornell, N., and Clarke, J. (1999). The cost of quality: Evaluating a standards-based design project. *National Association for Secondary School Principals Bulletin.* Retrieved December 15, 2006, from http://www.findarticles.com/p/articles/mi _qa3696/is_199901/ai_n8835892.

Corporation for National and Community Service. (2006). *College students helping America: Full report.* Retrieved July 15, 2008, from http:// www.mational/service. org/pdf/06_1016_RPO_college_full.pdf

Corporation for National and Community Service. (2008). *Performance highlights fiscal year 2007.* Retrieved July 5, 2008, from http://www.nationalservice.org/pdf/ afr_2007_highlights.pdf.

Davis, K. M., Miller, M. D., and Corbett, W. T. (1998). *Methods of evaluating student performance through service learning.* Gainesville: University of Florida. Retrieved July 13, 2008, from http://www.fsu.edu/~flserve/resources/evalmethods. html

Dewey, J. (1900/1990). *The school and society.* Chicago: University of Chicago Press.

Dewey, J. (1913). *Interest and effort in education.* New York, NY: Houghton Mifflin Company.

Dewey, J. (1916/1997). *Democracy and education: An introduction to the philosophy of education.* New York: Simon & Schuster.

Dewey, J. (1938a). *Experience and education.* New York: The Free Press.

Dewey, J. (1938b). *Logic: The theory of inquiry.* New York: Holt, Rinehart, and Winston.

Dewey, J. (1973a). Experience and philosophic method. In J. J. McDermott (Ed.), *The philosophy of John Dewey* (pp. 249–277). Chicago: University of Chicago Press. (Reprinted from Experience and Nature, chapter 1, by J. Dewey, 1958, New York.)

Dewey, J. (1973b). Interest in relation to the training of the will. In J. J. McDermott (Ed.), *The philosophy of John Dewey* (pp. 441–442). Chicago: University of Chicago Press. (Reprinted from second supplement to the *Herbart Year Book for 1895,* pp. 209–246, by J. Dewey, 1896, Bloomington, IL: National Herbart Society.)

Dewey, J. (1973c). Pattern of inquiry. In J. J. McDermott (Ed.). *The philosophy of John Dewey* (pp. 223–239). Chicago: University of Chicago Press. (Reprinted from

Logic: The theory of inquiry, pp. 101–119, by J. Dewey, 1938, Austin, TX: Holt, Rinehart, & Winston.)

Ebersole, M. M., and Worster, A. M. (2007). Sense of place in teacher preparation courses: Place-based and standards-based education. *Delta Kappa Gamma Bulletin, 73*(2), 19–24.

Eccles, J. S., and Wigfield, A. (1997). Young adolescent development. In J. L. Irvin (Ed.), *What current research says to the middle level practitioner* (pp. 15–29). Columbus, OH: National Middle School Association.

Exploratorium Institute for Inquiry. (2008a). *Pathways to learning: The Institute for Inquiry's approach to teaching and learning science through inquiry.* Retrieved July 20, 2008, from http://www.exploratorium.edu/IFI/docs/IFI_pathways_essay. pdf.

Exploratorium Institute for Inquiry. (2008b). *Inquiry structure for learning science content.* Retrieved July 20, 2008, from http://www.exploratorium.edu/IFI/about/ inquiry_structure.html

Fink, L. D. (2003). *Creating significant learning experiences.* San Francisco: Jossey-Bass.

Fullan, M. (2001). *The new meaning of educational change.* New York: Teachers College Press.

Furco, A. (1996). Service-learning: A balanced approach to experiential education. In *Expanding boundaries: Serving and learning* (pp. 2–6).Washington, DC: Corporation for National Service.

Furco, A., and Billig, S. H. (2002). *Service-learning: The essence of the pedagogy.* Greenwich, CT: Information Age Publishing.

Gardener, H. (1991). *The unschooled mind: How children think and how schools should teach.* New York: Basic Books.

Giesbrecht, S. (2008). The 100-mile curriculum: Place as an educative construct. *Education Canada, 48*(2), 26–29.

Gonzales, A. H., and Nelson, L. M. (2005). Learner centered instruction promotes student success. *The Journal, 32*(6), 10–15.

Graham, M. A. (2007). Art, ecology, and art education: Locating art education in a critical place-based pedagogy. *Studies in Art Education, 48*(4), 375–390.

Grant, M., and Branch, R. (2005). Project based learning in a middle school: Tracing abilities through the artifacts of learning. *Journal of Research on Technology in Education, 38*(1), 65–98.

Greene, J. P., and Winters, M. A. (2006). *The boys left behind: The gender graduation gap.* National Review. Retrieved June 6, 2007, from http://www.nationalreview. com/comment/greene_winters200604190558.asp.

Greunewald, D. A. (2003). Foundations of place: A multidisciplinary framework for place-conscious education. *American Educational Research Journal, 40*(3), 619–654.

Gupta, J. (2006). A model for interdisciplinary service-learning experience for social change. *Journal of Physical Therapy Education, 20*(3), 55–60.

Gutek, G. L. (1968). *Pestalozzi and education.* Prospect Heights, IL: Waveland Press.

Gutek, G. L. (1991). *An historical introduction to American education.* Prospect Heights, IL: Waveland Press.

Harmin, M. (1994). *Inspiring active learning: A handbook for teachers.* Alexandria, VA: Association for Supervision and Curriculum Development.

Harvard Documentation and Assessment Program. (2001). *Assessing student work.* Henderson, NC: Rural School and Community Trust.

Heinecke, W. F., Curry-Corcoran, D. E., and Moon, T. R. (2003). U.S. schools and the new standards and accountability initiative. In D. Duke, M. Grogan, P. Tucker, and W. Heinecke (Eds.), *Educational leadership in an age of accountability* (pp. 7–35). Albany, NY: State University of New York Press.

Hmelo-Silver, C. E. (2004). Problem-based learning: What and how do students learn? *Educational Psychology Review, 16*(3), 235–266.

Hmelo-Silver, C. E., Duncan, R. G., and Chinn, C. A. (2007). Scaffolding and achievement in problem-based and inquiry learning: A response to Kirschner, Sweller, and Clark (2006). *Educational Psychologist, 42*(2), 99–107.

Hoover, S. (2006). Popular culture in the classroom: Using video clips to enhance survey classes. *History Teacher, 39*(4), 467–478.

Huba, M. E., and Freed, J. E. (2000). *Learner-centered assessment on college campuses: Shifting the focus from teaching to learning.* Needham Heights, MA: Allyn & Bacon.

Hutchings, P., and Wutzdorff, A. (1988). Experiential learning across the curriculum: Assumptions and principles. In P. Hutchings and A. Wutzdorff (Eds.), *Knowing and doing: Learning through experience.* San Francisco: Jossey-Bass.

Igo, C., Moore, D. M., Ramsey, J., and Ricketts, J. C. (2008). The problem-solving approach. *Techniques, 83*(1), 52–55.

International Association for Research on Service-learning and Community Engagement. (2008). *Our history.* Retrieved July 16, 2008, from http://www.researchslce.org/_Files/Public_Site/About_Us_Files/history.htm.

International Partnership for Service-Learning and Leadership. (2008). *What is service learning?* Retrieved June 2, 2008, from http://www.ipsl.org/advocacy/declaration-of-principles.html.

Inquiry Learning Forum. (2008). *What is inquiry?* Retrieved July 20, 2008, from http://ilf.crlt.indiana.edu/.

Keeton, M. T. (1976). *Experiential learning.* San Francisco: Jossey-Bass.

Kilpatrick, W. (1918). The project method. *Teachers College Record, 19*(4), 319–335.

Kirschner, P. A., Sweller, J., and Clark, R. E. (2006). Why minimal guidance during instruction does not work: An analysis of the failure of constructivist, discover, problem-based, experiential, and inquiry-based teaching. *Educational Psychologist, 41*(2), 75–86.

Knapp, C. E. (2005). The "I-Thou" relationship, place-based education, and Aldo Leopold. *Journal of Experiential Education, 27*(3), 277–285.

Knoll, M. (1997). The project method: Its vocational education origin and international development. *Journal of Industrial Teacher Education, 34*(3), 59–80.

Kolb, D. A. (1984). *Experiential learning: Experience as the source of learning and development.* Englewood Cliffs, NJ: Prentice Hall.

Kraft, R., and Sakofs, M. (1984). *The theory of experiential education.* Boulder, CO: Association for Experiential Education.

Learn and Serve America. (2008a). *Six colleges and universities receive presidential award for exemplary community service.* Retrieved July 12, 2008, from http://www.learnandserve.gov/about/newsroom/releases_detail.asp?tbl_pr_id=950.

Learn and Serve America. (2008b). *What is Learn and Serve America?* Retrieved July 16, 2008, from http://www.learnandserve.gov/about/lsa/index.asp.

Learn and Serve America's National Service-Learning Clearinghouse. (2008). *What is service-learning.* Retrieved July 6, 2008, from http://www.servicelearning.org/what_is_service-learning/index.php.

Lee, S. Y., Olszewski-Kubilius, P., Donahue, R., and Weimholt, K. (2007). The effects of a service-learning program on the development of civic attitudes and behaviors among academically talented adolescents. *Journal for the Education of the Gifted, 31*(2), 165–197.

Leopold, A. (1949/1987). *Sand County almanac.* Oxfordshire, UK: Oxford University Press.

Levine, E. (2002). *One kid at a time: Big lessons from a small school.* New York: Teachers College Press.

Levine, A., and Cureton, J. S. (1998). *When hope and fear collide: A portrait of today's college student.* San Francisco: Jossey-Bass.

Levitz, R., Noel, L., and Richter, B. (1999). Strategic moves for retention success. *New Directions for Higher Education, 27*(4), 31–49.

Littky, D., and Grabelle, S. (2004). *The big picture: Education is everyone's business.* Alexandria, VA: Association for Supervision and Curriculum Development.

Liu, M., and Hsiao, Y. (2002). Middle school students as multimedia designers: A project-based learning approach. *Journal of Interactive Learning Research, 13*(4), 311–337.

Lopez, R., Campbell, R., and Jennings, J. (2008). *Schoolyard improvements and standardized test scores: An ecological analysis.* Mauricio Gaston Institute for Latino Community Development and Public Policy. University of Massachusetts, Boston. Retrieved August 20, 2008, from http://www.peecworks.org/PEEC/PEEC_Research/03070B26–007EA7AB.0/Lopez%20Campbell%20Jennings%202008%20schoolyards%20and%20test%20scores.pdf.

Louv, R. (2005). *Last child in the woods: Saving our children from nature-deficit disorder.* Chapel Hill, NC: Algonquin Books.

Louv, R. (2007, March/April). Leave no child inside. *Orion Magazine, 2.* Retrieved August 6, 2008, from http://www.orionmagazine.org/index.php/articles/article/240

Lucas, G. (2007). What's next. *NEA Today, 25*(8), 25.

Machemer, P. L., & Crawford, P. (2007). *Active Learning in Higher Education, 8*(1), 9–30.

Markham, T., Larmer, J., and Ravitz, J. (2003). *Project based learning handbook: A guide to standards-focused project based learning for middle and high school teachers.* Novato, CA: Buck Institute for Education.

Martin, L. A. (2005). Use of cognitive strategies by high school social studies students. *Action in Teacher Education, 26*(4), 63–73.

McDermott, J. J. (Ed.). (1981). *The philosophy of John Dewey.* Chicago: University of Chicago Press.

McMaster University Medical School. (2008). *What is PBL?* Retrieved July 20, 2008, from http://chemeng.mcmaster.ca/pbl/pbl.htm.

Messineo, M., Gaither, G., Bott, J., & Ritchey, K. (2007). Inexperienced versus experienced students' expectations for active leaning in large classes. *College Teaching,* 55(3), 125–33.

Meyers, C., and Jones, T. B. (1993). *Promoting active learning: Strategies for the college classroom.* San Francisco: Jossey-Bass.

Middendorf, J., and Kalish, A. (1996). The change up in lectures. *The National Teaching and Learning Forum, 5*(2). Retrieved February28,2009, from http://www.ntlf.com/html/pi/9601/article1.htm.

Moore, K. D. (2009). *Effective instructional strategies.* Los Angeles: Sage.

National Environmental Education and Training Foundation. (2000). *Environment-based education: Creating high performance schools and students.* Washington, DC: Author. Retrieved August 20, 2008, from http://www.neefusa.org/pdf/NEETF8400.pdf.

National Park Service. (2008). *Youth Conservation Corps.* Retrieved July 16, 2008, from http://www.nps.gov/gettinginvolved/youthprograms/ycc.htm.

National Society for Experiential Education Foundations Document. (1997). *Standards of practice: Eight principles of good practice for all experiential learning activities.* Retrieved on February 28, 2009, from http://www.nsee.org/about_us.htm#mission.

Nelson, J. A., and Eckstein, D. (2008). A service-learning model for at-risk adolescents. *Education and Treatment of Children, 31*(2), 223–227.

Newell, R. (2003). *Passion for learning: How project based learning meets the needs of 21st-century students.* Lanham, MD: The Scarecrow Press.

Newell, R. (2007). Project-based learning. Unpublished manuscript.

Newman, M. (2003). *A pilot systematic review and meta-analysis on the effectiveness of problem-based learning.* Campbell Collaboration Systematic Review Group. Retrieved December 12, 2005, from http://www.ltsn-01.ac.uk/docs/pbl_report.pdf.

No Child Left Inside Coalition. (2009). Retrieved February 22, 2009, from Chesapeake Bay Foundation website: http://www.cbf.org/page.aspx?pid=687.

Pearlman, B. (2009). *New skills for a new century: Students thrive on cooperation and problem solving.* Retrieved on January 22, 2009, from http://www.edutopia.org/new-skills-new-century.

Place-based Education Evaluation Collaborative. (2003). *PEEC overview paper.* Retrieved July 23, 2008, from http://www.peecworks.org/index.

Place-Based Landscape Analysis and Community Education. (2008). *Tips and techniques for exploring place.* Retrieved August 20, 2008, from http://www.promiseofplace.org/resources_curriculum/documents/ReadingtheLandscapeIntro.pdf.

Popham, W. J. (2008). *Transformative assessment.* Alexandria, VA: Association for Supervision and Curriculum Development.

Powers, A. L. (2004). Evaluation of four place-based education programs. *Journal of Environmental Education, 35*(4), 17–32.

Powers, A., and PEER Associates. (2008*). PEEC research brief #1: Service-learning.* Retrieved Aug 20, 2008, from http://www.peecworks.org/PEEC/PEEC_Reports/0344F22E-007EA7AB.0/Service%20Learning%20Research%20Brief%20v3c.pdf.

Problem-Based Learning Network. (2008). *PBLN-IMSA overview.* Retrieved July 18, 2008, from http://www.imsa.edu/programs/pbln/overview/mission.php.

Promise of Place. (2008a). *What is place-based education?* Retrieved July 23, 2008, from http://promiseofplace.org/what_is_pbe.

Promise of Place. (2008b). *How place-based education works.* Retrieved July 24, 2008, from http://www.promiseofplace.org/how_pbe_works/.

Railsback, J. (2002*). Project-based instruction: Creating excitement for learning.* Portland, OR: Northwest Regional Educational Laboratory.

Ruitenberg, C. (2005). Deconstructing the experience of the local: Toward a radical pedagogy of place. In *Philosophy of Education Yearbook* (pp. 12–20). New York: H. W. Wilson.

Rural School and Community Trust. (2003). *Documenting and assessing place-based learning: Example portfolios.* Retrieved July 31, 2008, from http://portfolio.ruraledu.org/.

Sarkar, S., and Frazier, R. (2008). Place-based investigations and authentic inquiry. *The Science Teacher, 75*(2), 29–33.

Savery, J. (2006). Overview of problem-based learning: Definitions and distinctions. *Interdisciplinary Journal of Problem-based Learning, 1*(1), 9–20.

Sax, L. J., Keup, J. R., Gilmartin, S. K., Stolzenberg, E. B., and Harper, C. (2002). *Findings from the 2000 administration of "Your First College Year": National aggregates.* Los Angeles: University of California, Higher Education Research Institute.

Schmidt, H. G., Loyens, S. M., Van Gog, T., and Paas, F. (2007). Problem-based learning is compatible with human cognitive architecture: Commentary on Kirschner, Sweller, and Clark (2006). *Educational Psychologist, 42*(2), 91–97.

Schroeder, C. C. (1993). New students — new learning styles. *Change, 25*(4), 21–26.

Senior Corps. (2008). *What is Senior Corps?* Retrieved July 14, 2008, from http://www.seniorcorps.org/about/sc/index.asp.

Shaller, M. (2005, July-August). Wandering and wondering: Traversing the uneven terrain of the second college year. *About Campus, 10*(3). Retrieved on February 26, 2009, from http://www3.interscience.wiley.com/journal/110568792/issue.

Shedd, J. M. (2003). The history of the student credit hour. *New Directions for Higher Education, 122*, 5–12.

Smith, G. A. (2002). Place-based education: Learning to be where we are. *Phi Delta Kappan, 83*(8), 584–594.

Sobel, D. (2005). *Place-based education: Connecting classrooms and communities.* Great Barrington, MA: The Orion Society.

Sobel, D. (2008). *Childhood and nature: Design principles for educators.* Portland, ME: Stenhouse.

Stavrianopoulos, K. (2008). Service learning within the freshman year experience. *College Student Journal, 42*(2), 703–712.

Stiggins, R. J., Arter, J. A., Chappuis, J., and Chappuis, S. (2006). *Classroom assessment for student learning.* Princeton, NJ: Educational Testing Services.

Strong, R. W., Silver, H. F., and Perini, M. J. (2001). *Teaching what matters most: Standards and strategies for raising student achievement.* Alexandria, VA: Association for Supervision and Curriculum Development.

Svinicki, M. D. (2007). Moving beyond "it worked": The ongoing evolution of research on problem-based learning in medical education. *Educational Psychology Review, 19*(1), 49–61.

Sweller, J. (2004). Instructional design consequences of an analogy between evolution by natural selection and human cognitive architecture. *Instructional Science, 32*(1/2), 9–31.

Sweller, J., Kirschner, P. A., and Clark, R. E. (2007). Why minimally guided teaching techniques do not work: A reply to commentaries. *Educational Psychologist, 42*(2), 115–121.

Swick, K. (2001). Nurturing decency through caring and serving during the early childhood years. *Early Childhood Education Journal, 29*(2), 131–137.

Thomas, D., Enloe, W., and Newell, R. (2005). *The coolest school in America.* Lanham, MD: Scarecrow Education.

Titlebaum, P., Williamson, G., Daprano, C., Baer, J., and Brahler, J. (2004). *Annotated history of service learning.* Retrieved on June 10, 2008, from http://www. servicelearning.org/filemanager/download/142/SL%20Comp%20Timeline%203–15-04_rev.pdf.

University of Colorado at Boulder Service-Learning Office. (2008). *Mission of Service-Learning Office.* Retrieved May 15, 2008, from http://www.colorado.edu/ servicelearning/index.html.

U.S. Department of Education. (2008). *Four pillars of NCLB.* Retrieved August 5, 2008, from http://www.ed.gov/nclb/overview/intro/4pillars.html.

Warner-Weil, S., and McGill, I. (1989). *Making sense of experiential learning: Diversity in theory and practice.* Bristol, PA: Open University Press.

White, H. (1995, January). "Creating problems" for PBL. *Newsletter of the Center for Teaching Effectiveness, 47.* University of Delaware. Retrieved July 23, 2008, from http://www.udel.edu/pbl/cte/jan95–chem.html.

Wilderness Society. (2008). *About the Wilderness Society.* Retrieved August 10, 2008, from http://wilderness.org/about-us/history.

Wolk, R. A. (2001). Bored of education. *Teacher Magazine, 13*(3), 3.

Wurdinger, S., Haar, J., Hugg, B., and Bezon, J. (2007). A qualitative study using project based learning in a mainstream middle school. *Improving Schools, 10*(2), 150–161.

Wurdinger, S. D. (2005). *Using experiential learning in the classroom: Practical ideas for all educators.* Lanham, MD: Scarecrow Education.

Wurdinger, S. D., & Rdolph, J. L. (2009). A different type of success: Teaching important life skills through project-based learning. *Improving Schools,* 12(2), 117–131.

Youth Learn. (2008). *How to develop an inquiry based project.* Retrieved July 20, 2008, from http://www.youthlearn.org/learning/activities/howto.asp.

About the Authors

Scott D. Wurdinger is professor of experiential education and leadership studies in the College of Education, Department of Educational Leadership, Minnesota State University, Mankato. He has been teaching in higher education for twenty years.

Julie A. Carlson's career as an educator spans more than three decades of outdoor, adventure, and experiential learning endeavors. She is a faculty member in the Department of Educational Leadership at Minnesota State University, Mankato.